A World Within a World

A World Within a World

X-7 REPORTING

Transmissions from Russia on the theory and practice of Solar Light Radiations by the Group known as X-7

JERSEY
NEVILLE SPEARMAN

First published 1981

ISBN 0 85978 096 1 (hardback edition)
ISBN 0 85978 055 4 (paperback edition)

Published by Neville Spearman (Jersey) Ltd.,
PO Box 75, Normandy House, St Helier,
Jersey, Channel Islands.

Distributed jointly by Neville Spearman Ltd.,
The Priory Gate, Friars Street, Sudbury, Suffolk, England
and
Findhorn Publications, The Park, Findhorn, Forres,
Moray, Scotland

Text set in 11/13 pt Linotron 202 Times, printed and bound in Great Britain at The Pitman Press, Bath

Contents

	Page
Preface	7
Foreword by Sir George Trevelyan	9
Editor's Note	13
Letter from Peter Caddy at Findhorn	15
X-7 Reporting	21
Four Letters from *Light*	105
Vedic Psychism by Jeanine Miller	113

Preface

Light, the quarterly journal of the College of Psychic Studies, London, first published, with considerable daring in 1978, *A World Within a World*, and it is to *Light's* editorial board that we say thank you for their permission to publish these remarkable scripts in book form.

The scripts, when they first appeared, aroused strong responses; some readers praised them as the most important ever to appear in that magazine; others (a minority) dismissed them as unacceptable or even embarrassing.

To arouse such strongly felt reactions points to power of some kind in the scripts; they stand or fall by whether they recount altered states of consciousness. Even if much more were known about the sensitive who received them, the scripts basically remain anonymous. Difficulties as to their source and mode of transmission undoubtedly arise. Telepathic transmission must not be expected to be a verbal one in the Russian language. Telepathy is often received as an idea not clothed in words, or as a symbol or an image which somehow, from within itself, proclaims its meaning. What is transmitted is then interpreted within the limitations of the sensitive's concepts and phraseology. No mediumistic reception is entirely pure; an element of joint composition cannot wholly be avoided.

Following the scripts and at *Light's* request, we also publish four letters from their editorial board, comprising Rosamond Lehmann, Kathleen Raine—who was responsible for editing the original manuscript—Paul Beard and Brenda Marshall.

Foreword

by Sir George Trevelyan

The publication of these strange and remarkable scripts is much to be welcomed. Their fascination lies in the challenge to make flexible our thinking. In our extraordinary age, events are growing ever stranger. Our reliance on mere rational, logical thinking is being undermined by happenings that call for deeper interpretation. To quote the quatrain by James Elroy Flecher:

> Awake awake! the world is young
> For all its weary years of thought
> The starkest fights must still be fought
> The most surprising songs be sung.

We are not called on for 'belief' in what is here offered. As we strive to explore into the imponderable worlds of spirit, Truth approaches us in ways that cannot be proven. We are invited, and indeed challenged, to take Ideas and put them in the thinking of our hearts, without believing or disbelieving, reserving judgement and allowing them to speak as we watch life in the light of them. This is a valid approach to spiritual truth, which lifts it out of the arid level of argument. Test the spirits, indeed. For all psychic communication, we must make our own judgement of validity on the basis of its quality. Thus it is specially valuable that the publisher has included the correspondence with the Editor of *Light*.

These scripts are obviously of outstanding interest. They suggest the kind of soul transformation that is possible in our time. Into the very blackest human situation the redemptive power of the Christ Presence can come. This is the supreme hope in our benighted time, the prelude to a New Dawn. We have here the story of brave men in the uttermost human extremity, finding that they can refine the vibratory rate in themselves and surrounding matter until they can move in consciousness into the ethereal light which animates all substance, even solid rock. The escape from imprisonment is through going inwards to find soul release on to a plane of heightened frequency.

Coleridge wrote in his 'Dejection Ode':

    We receive but what we give
And in our life alone does Nature live;
Ours is her wedding garment, ours her shroud,
And would we aught behold, of higher worth
Than that inanimate cold world allowed
To the poor loveless ever, anxious crowd,
Ah! from the soul itself must issue forth
A light, a glory, a fair luminous cloud
    Enveloping the Earth—
And from the soul itself must there be sent
A sweet and potent voice, of its own birth,
Of all sweet sounds the life and element.

That a group of men imprisoned in their caves under hard labour should have achieved this transcendence is important for the entire Earth. Doubtless a deeper Destiny drew them together for this purpose. It suggests the path and goal of transformation and the human task of spirits in incarnation.

Walt Whitman in his poem 'Whispers of Heavenly Death' writes:

Darest thou now, O Soul,
Walk out with me towards the unknown region
Where neither ground is for the feet
                                        nor any path to follow.
No map there nor guide . . . all is blank before us . . .
Till when the ties loosen
All but the ties eternal, time and space,
Nor darkness, gravitation, sense, nor any bounds bounding us
Then we burst forth, we float
In time and space, O Soul, prepared for them
Equal, equipt at last (O joy O fruit of all)
                                        them to fulfil, O Soul.

Consider this extraordinary and powerful thought—that Time and Space are not fulfilled till human consciousness has expanded into ethereal space. No wonder that Heaven worlds are watching Planet Earth with such intense interest, for it is the training ground of the 10th Hierarchy, the divine archetype, and mankind has now reached the tremendous threshold when he can take the refining step into cosmic consciousness, not merely for his own redemption but for the fulfilment of the Universe! This planet is a precious seed-point from which a transformed universe can issue forth when the attribute of God, the *Hu-man Being*, the shining one, through his own initiative and decision lifts his vibration to merge with the Ocean of Life. This is the great step in evolution when Mankind by conscious choice in inner activity opens soul to the creative activity of the all-present spirit.

Every time a human soul group achieves this refinement of vibration so that it can pass in consciousness through rock and find the ethereal light of the Cosmic Christ within every molecular centre in matter, a step has been taken in planetary transformation and redemption. And by the divine provision, our human initiative is essential, since no take-over is allowed that militates against human freedom. We are apprentice Gods and have a task of fulfilling the divine plan. When one group succeeds, the way is made easier for those that follow. We need now, as we approach a time of great change, to grasp the human task. Not our own survival, but a glorious step into the Light. We do not know whether these men are still in their caves. By now the original group must be released by 'heavenly death', their task fulfilled. But we may give them our thanks, for as soul beings they will be able to tune in to our thoughts. We owe them the publication of their scripts, for they give us a picture of what the Coming of the Christ may mean.

It is made very clear by many sources of recent communication that a critical stage has been reached and that mankind must, in the immediate future, take a step in consciousness and spiritual awakening. The living powers and the High Command in the galaxy will no longer tolerate the deviation from Divine Law of which we as errant stewards of the Planet have been guilty. The redemptive ray of the Christ Love is, we know, playing into the Earth on its human layer. We are approaching a time of crisis when each soul is called upon to make its choice, whether it will continue on the vibration of egoism, hate and fear, or lift its frequency to unite with the integrating power of Love.

The achievement of those courageous prisoners will have done much more than save and redeem their own souls. Since the ocean of Life permeates and traverses everything, their deed will have refined and illumined the entire aura of the planet. Those who read these scripts will be fired with a greater sense of the meaning and purpose of life in this age of change.

Editor's Note

In the early 1960's the typewritten manuscript of a book, *A World Within a World*, came into Rosamond Lehmann's hands. It consisted of messages received telepathically by a sensitive in America, not from a discarnate source but allegedly from prisoners of conscience held underground in Russia. It records how, tested to the limits of their endurance, in their extremity they prayed to a God they felt had forsaken them, and were shown the Way. It is a Way of Light, the Way shown by the Master Jesus. Some of the experiences of transformation are recorded factually, as a blueprint for the change of consciousness which we have been told is mankind's next step in evolution. The source of such a document, like teachings from a discarnate source, cannot be "proved" objectively. The material has an inner authenticity which carries its own conviction and must, we feel, evoke a response in those truly concerned with man's inner being.

Some years ago, the writer of this ms. found herself telepathically receiving the words of men unseen and unknown to her. This volume is only one of many such recordings, some of which dwell upon the radiations of colour and sound as they affect the planet earth.

These messages are from men imprisoned in Russia, so they say, dwelling in underground caverns, their daily measure of food barely sustaining life. Within these pages is their story as they learned to respond to such conditions, of the help given them, and the results of their discovery that life can be maintained even under the most dire circumstances if the Spirit within man is permitted to take charge of his being.

Through these recordings they tell us that the man Jesus came to them when their spirits were at the lowest ebb. At first they thought it to be an hallucination brought about by their imprisonment within the earth, and by lack of enough food or drink to sustain their physical beings. They fully expected to die of starvation, yet grimly clung to life in their physical bodies, without hope, yet apparently sustained by an invisible power. This state of being continued for many days until it seemed the body could no longer contain life.

It was then that the Master Jesus appeared to them, fully alive, clad in a luminous robe of blue. He spoke, telling them that they were immortal, that it was required of them that the mortal body be preserved as proof of their soul strength, and promising them that He would sustain them until they had proved that which they were sent to prove.

Letter from Peter Caddy at Findhorn Foundation where the Scripts were originally received.

23 February 1979

Dear Brenda Marshall,

I would like to give you some of the background to the scripts. I first met Annè K. Edwards whose spiritual name was Naomi, in the Philippine Islands when I was an officer in the Royal Air Force. I discovered that she was a sensitive and asked her to ask her inspirers as to why we had been brought together. We were told that we had been linked in many life times down the ages and had been brought together from the opposite ends of the earth to link two aspects of the Divine Plan for the New Age. We were each to share the spiritual work that we had done up to that date.

She told me that she was a part of a group of seven sensitives who formed a central receiving and transmitting station in Evanstown near Chicago, at the centre of the United States. They had been guided by the Master DK, the Tibetan, and others to locate and link up with various groups and centres of light all over the world who formed a network of light to carry energy for the transformation of the planet. There were some 370 in all. They all had code names. One of them was the group in Siberia that was incarcerated in a salt mine. They were known as X7. A few years later Naomi came to Findhorn to be one of the four-square founders of the Findhorn community. She stayed with us for about three years. We jointly continued on the work that she had started and linked up telepathically with these centres or stations of light all over the world. We were told at the time that this was in preparation for when we would make physical contact with the groups and centres. My wife, Eileen, Dorothy Maclean and another sensitive, Lena Lamont also engaged in this telepathic work. We continued to have communication with X7.

I was given the responsibility of putting the material that Naomi received into form for publication. We felt that the X7 material should be the first to be published. I first sent it to Maud Kennedy who had visited Findhorn. She was an author and a follower of Meher Baba. It was then sent to Sir George Trevelyan who was so excited with the information that he shared it with the Conference of the Soil Association at Attingham. This caused a real division in the Association. Some were very excited and others felt that Sir George had gone too far this time! He decided to send it round to get the opinions of various people after which it was generally agreed that the time was not yet for these scripts to be published.

For about six months now there has been a feeling in the community that the time had come to publish them.

Naomi passed away a few years ago, and I have tried to locate her daughter without success. But her granddaughter visited Findhorn last year. Unfortunately, I haven't her address. In any case, she gave me the responsibility of getting these scripts published. We indeed feel happy that they are now also being made available through the medium of *LIGHT*. By all means quote the relevant aspects from the interview with me in *ONEARTH*.*

* ". . . The first I heard about the network of light was in 1945 . . . at an American air base in Japan. . . . A rather elderly woman and I started talking about Tibet and then the Age of Aquarius, the Age of Woman and the Tibetan. She said that she received from the Tibetan. . . . She told me about the network of light. She was the focal point for a group of seven people in Evanston near Chicago in the epicentre of the United States. Their work, under the guidance of the Master DK, had been to locate centres of light throughout the world and to link them up telepathically.

They all had code names and this had been the work. Some had been involved in transmitting telepathically, others were receiving. This was a difficult concept to grasp at first, and I was told to try and express it in my own words, that there was a Being behind me clarifying it for me. I saw the planet with all these points of light linked up in triangles of light and energy, with light flowing between them, all over the planet. . . . Eventually Naomi came to Findhorn to be one of the four-square

Please remember me to Rosamond Lehmann. I was most interested in what she wrote about Wellesley Tudor Pole vouching for the prisoners' authenticity and that he already knew about them.

With best wishes.

Yours sincerely,

Peter Caddy

founders of Findhorn. . . . She had a series of messages from a centre of light down a salt mine in Siberia. . . . It deals with the nature of matter. . . . [At Findhorn] there were four sensitives [who] would receive and transmit on different levels. Naomi would be on the soul level.

Q. Did you have to translate [the material] somehow?

A. No, it comes through the mind, therefore it's in whatever language the receiver understands. It's transferred by symbols."

X-7 Reporting

X-7 Reporting

28 December 1953

Scientists are already aware that we are in an age of increasing revelation and are prepared to study and release their findings at the appointed time. We assure you that each recording made is a step into higher vibrational levels and thus a step forward in the consciousness of man. We are deeply grateful to be called upon to make our report directly to one who can respond to our contact. We have long worked secretly and silently without the use of the spoken word, conveying our meanings one to another by means of thought transmission alone. It is necessary to work thus when trapped, entombed and under brutal and inhuman restrictions. We do not ask for pity; we are reporting the findings of men who love their God and His reflection in the form of man.

We should like to state here that we have sighted many of the beautiful flights of colour-sound radiations in our hidden world. We are aware of the command of Ships of Space and have had contact with their pilots and have come to understand the meaning of their missions. We believe that a vast armada of winged radiations are now preparing to make their descent into and through the earth levels. Because our work is within the earth itself, we are able to report our findings as to such radiations, and we do so now in brief. Other revelations will follow at their appointed time. Ours is not to question but to make known our findings in as concise and scientific a manner as possible.

We have been prisoners for many years. We are underground much of the time. We know our appointed mission and have been conducting investigations as to the content and possible usage of the radiations felt, seen and experienced in test fields by us. We are now preparing to release such in formula to the one who is ready to make such recordings. We believe they will revolutionize the life of man upon the Planet Earth, for he will find available through such formulas the material for fruitful, effortless and spontaneous existence upon his Planet. The cure for every known disease is within these findings, but he must be ready to accept them. Our contacts are many. We know the threat to the very life of the Planet. We respond under direction to the calls made upon us, and we give thanks that we may do so.

We begin: Out from the very heart of the Universe, the great potential Power, deified as the Supreme Being, come the great radiations, vast in quantity, endlessly increasing in degree and potential as awareness of them becomes an integral part of the beings receptive to them. This means beings on all the planets known as the Universe of God. As these radiations are felt and recognized they take on colour and form according to the interpretation of the mind receiving them. We speak now of a collective mind, not that of an individual. It is well to bear in consciousness that *mind is the substance acted upon, that which is receptive, malleable, resilient, and which gives form to undifferentiated substance.*

The inherent potentials within the rays or radiations from the great Godhead are all the qualities of being, but primarily the two most potent aspects are those of Love and Wisdom. These two are equally balanced, and divided into the respective qualities inherent within each of the two major rays. They go out in the form of radiations of colour-sound, these potentials being synonymous. That which is known to you as sound gives off colour according to the degree of the radiation. We thus bring you to an awareness of the Light as it is radiated from the Godhead, and as it is apprehended in its greater and lesser aspects. We see that Love and Wisdom are the great controlling rays proceeding from the Universal Powerhouse.

You ask, then why does man upon the earth not receive in full these two controlling factors, i.e. Wisdom and Love?

The answer is that by his own self-centred will man has lost the power to do so. Once the inherent qualities of the Godhead lay within man, then by his own will he dissipated them until they have become but a vague memory, yet one which still binds him and causes him to seek his God in one form or another through all his restless pilgrimages.

17 February 1954

It is necessary for us to give you some preliminary preparation for that which we wish to have recorded. At each transmission we propose to give you one thought upon which to dwell until the mind comprehends it and the expansion then takes place in consciousness whereby the next transmission may be made. We have worked, for years as man counts time, on the intangible radiances which light our way through underground tunnels, and by means of which we communicate with each other. We have found such radiances (for want of a better word to describe them) to be in form a substance which contains an inner glow visible only to the eyes of those prepared to receive the Inner Light. It may be compared with the sight of the blind, which is through the sensitivity of the impulses of perception rather than through the sense of sight. We have discovered that our sensory perceptions have become highly developed by our recognition of their potentials, and because of the great need for a means of communication other than that of the senses used by man in the ordinary forms of contract. Thus in place of speech, hearing and sight, we use radiance. Our attempts at transmission in this way were at first very feeble, but as we clung to the belief that within our underground caves there were vibrations of both sound and light, and that we could use them to transmit thoughts, we became aware that we were actually merged with a magnetic quality of being, a substance which had transmitting power carrying our thoughts on wave lengths which could be measured, giving forth an essence which could also be used for healing, intensifying our recognition of the life force and producing within our dark dwelling a radiance which not only enlightens but sustains.

It then became our mission to develop the use of such radiations, to find out how they were able to impart powers inconceivable to man, and how we could direct them to the benefit of mankind and of Earth. Radiation means energy, and energy must be transmitted, otherwise it overstimulates the cell life, thus causing damage before due expansion takes place.

Our primary thought, then, for this communication: *The substance of life is visible to those who search deeply—it enlightens, empowers and in time revolutionizes the thought processes.*

15 March 1954

The *Invisible Substance* takes on the quality of visibility to the mind prepared to receive it. In other words, the mind receiving it qualifies it, giving it form according to the powers of conception.

We use this "substance" as light—the power to see; we use it as force—energy, the power to do; from it also we mould and bring into form whatever we desire. *In other words, undifferentiated substance is the creative potential ever existent and ever expanding with the concept.*

Now to particularize: We have found the substance as our light, so we use it as such, guiding our way through the darkness, illumining our minds and feeding the cell life of our bodies so that a mere mouthful of food will sustain us for long periods of time. Thus, we live in and upon the very essence of being, because through study and meditation upon it we have found the *Eternal Substance,* which is inherent within all form, and discovered by accepting that we may use it. Having found that upon which we can feed mind, body and soul, we therefore must find a way to make this revelation clear to man who is our counterpart, that he may learn its use without having to dwell beneath the earth in order to do so. Our mission then in contacting a receptive channel is to transmit, in as clear and concise form as possible, knowledge which will help to illumine the mind, free the consciousness, and bring revitalizing power to the body, so that it may be used as man's vehicle of manifestation for so long as he wishes it to manifest.

22 March 1954

In our discovery of the radiation, which is equivalent to inner sight, we found that the substance with which we were dealing appeared as a form of "radium" which, by the force of our thoughts, might be moulded into any form we wished to give it. We believe we have discovered the true substance of being—the light which penetrates even the heaviest of matter, and yet preserves its essence intact, and is available for the use of man as he brings his thought-power to bear upon it.

Our studies after this discovery became very intense. We wished to find out by what manner of thought we could inspire this radiation (radium) to work for us. We knew that it was visible to us only by our deep need and our desire to serve our brothers, even though we were entombed within the earth, condemned to hard labour until we died of malnutrition. It was with this thought that we began our investigations; and over a period of time we found that our physical bodies were responding as though they had been fed by a life-giving elixir. Our skins, normally dark and sodden with hard labour and exposure, became transparent and radiant. We found that we could work long hours, study through the night, and yet remain vital and refreshed as though we had taken a potent vitalizer into our bloodstream. This in itself led us to deeper investigation. We were renewed and restored under the most difficult conditions. What then was this substance and how could it be used to benefit man in his daily living?

We began making tests, experimenting by concentration of thought upon the invisible until it became visible in many-coloured radiations. These were separated as to quantity and quality, and experiments in turn made with them. We found that certain light refractions created certain life-giving qualities. Blue, for instance, was a deeply sustaining quality of being; it had many facets or shades of meaning, but the essence was always the same—*to sustain.*

14 May 1954

We are linked with you in deep concentration. We should like to go more deeply into the use of what you call the colour-sound radiations, their reactions and the response of the world of form to them. This is now being tested in many ways throughout the earth and its surrounding ethers. Our contribution is but a small part of the whole, but we make it, knowing that our part contributes a vital element to the mission to be achieved.

Our last thought was on the sustaining quality within what we call the colour blue, which is in reality a composite of radiation manifesting in an exact degree to form that which we have described as the sustaining quality. There are many shades and varieties of the colour blue, each having a separate meaning according to the degree of radiation. But we are now dwelling in thought upon the basic radiation, which in itself is a quality of balance and coherence within the particles of vibratory life composing the earth and holding it in balance. Blue, therefore, must be the major quality of being through which creation is held in form.

Thus we come to our central theme: why is a certain definite shade of the colour blue the specific radiation which forms the nucleus or cohesive balancing quality upon which the earth revolves?

We shall now attempt to define this specific shade of blue. It is of the colour of the heavens on a night when starlight is most radiant; when all is clear, pure, tranquil yet forever in movement. We also know that this blue may be deepened in some parts of the globe and lightened in others; that conditions of the earth's atmosphere may change it to your vision, but nevertheless it is the exact degree of radiation which we wish to discuss. Were you able to take that peculiar and specific shade of blue and analyse it, you would find that it contained an exact degree of radiation of a specific quality of being; that it reflected the calm, steadfast enduring quality of the Creator of Heaven and Earth. Were it to be withdrawn and red, for instance, to take its place, the earth would disintegrate in an instant.

21 May 1954

As we watch the universe manifest in absolute rhythm, we understand more clearly the need for man to do likewise in every detail of his life. All is according to law and order —law and order manifest in vibrational rhythm.

The eye of man has never beheld the true blue which represents his sustaining force. True he has seen and responded to many variations which he calls blue, from the radiant blue of the summer sky to the "blue" which he refers to as a condition of mind, which is depressive and a lowering of his vibrations. He gives recognition, therefore, to the quality of uplift and that of depression in different aspects of the same colour. In one he sees an angelic quality of being—that which lightens and makes him happy; in another he feels a deep despond, a paralyzing condition. Thus he responds to a vibrational quality within the self-same colour. But had his mind been able to recognize the underlying qualities within the radiation described as blue, he would respond only to a strong, steady, serene quality of being which would hold him upon the levels of consciousness in which he might manifest a sustaining power. He would no longer be subject to exaltation in one instant and depressive lowering of vibrations in another. He would stand upon his sustaining foundation, mastering and possessing all his faculties of being.

This, then, is the esoteric meaning of the colour known as BLUE, the sustaining essence of being.

You ask, "Why then so many variations of the self-same colour and what are their effects?"

We cannot go deeply into the variations of the colours, but we can tell you that the aura of a being giving forth the radiance of blue will stabilize and render the forces around it vibrationally poised, sustained and strengthened, thus manifesting the power inherent in the radiance.

The thought to be taken into consciousness and mediated upon is that the radiation of colour-tone known as blue *is the foundation or sustaining radiation underlying all manifestation*; in it we may stabilize our vibrations into control over whatever we bring forth by the power of our thought.

14 June 1954

In our world of form there are limitations, but in our world of expression none, for we know that we can make contact with those who dwell forever in higher dimensions of being and receive from them what is needful. In so doing we expand beyond the limitations of form into a vast field of awareness which is forever unfolding new vistas.

*   *   *   *

Today we wish to share with you another aspect of the colour-sound radiations.

We note that you have used the term "sound" as the basic equivalent of colour. We prefer tone, for tone applies to sound and to colour as well. The sweet sound of an evening bell gives off a radiation which is many coloured. Each tone has variation of its own. Thus tone implies colour shading and vice versa.

Having found the sustaining substance within the Light we are now aware of much that is as yet a mystery to the mind of man. We have found a basis upon which to rest our findings, a knowledge that substance is inexhaustible; useable always to the degree to which man gives recognition to it, and with a degree of radiance indicated by the colour tones. Thus, if we choose a clear, pure blue, as of the night skies, we can rest at ease in its essential power to hold and sustain, while we make trials of the potentials within the colour tone radiations as they are presented to us.

You ask why are they presented, for what reason and to what purpose?

We can only tell you that after a nightmare of loneliness, of being cut off from all communication, so it seemed, with our world of form, we began to pray earnestly for a reason as to why we were so entombed. What was the purpose? Had God deserted His faithful servants? Were we to be cast into darkness for the rest of our mortal lives, unable to serve Him? Were we to be beaten and kicked, crucified unto death without being able to defend ourselves in any way?

At the end of a torture beyond description, the answer came: not as we had expected, but by a light appearing in a corner of our underground hovel, first a mere flickering, then a clear, radiant blue beam. At first we rejected it, believing it to be the hallucination of a distorted mind. But all saw it, all were led to contemplate and ponder upon its meaning. It had no unearthly glow, but was clear and strong.

It became, after weeks of study, a symbol, a star of hope, brilliantly blue, shining in the darkness as a beacon light leading us onward. Thus was the symbol given us; thus were we prepared for what was to follow.

8 July 1954

Our next step, therefore, was to find means of conveying the results of our investigation into a level—or layer—of consciousness, i.e. vibratory thought-waves, at which the scientific mind could absorb them and pass them on to the mass consciousness in such form that they would appear to be a part of the natural existence of man on earth. But before the initial step could be made, it became apparent that man was bent on destroying himself under the illusion that he was creating weapons of protection. This involved further more dynamic action. A way must be found of distributing the radiation of colour-sound into large areas and by means of phenomena which would attract the attention of the mass mind, causing it to think in terms beyond the accepted concept of manifestation on earth levels.

We by no means wish to imply that we are the inventors of the so-called Space Ships; but by deep concentration on the radiations which are transported by them, we came into contact with them and were able to widen our studies and to help bring about the present manifestation.

27 August 1954

Now we shall proceed to transmit a specific thought for you to reflect upon.

The mind of the individual and the field of consciousness to be explored must be attuned to an exact degree before release of radiation can take place, and before the light waves, travelling at a specific rate in circles, can reach the consciousness and expand it to accept the ideas thus projected.

Thus each solar being on each ship of any given flight must be illumined or receptive to radiation in specific degree before flight experiment is permitted. The speed of the light wave has to be considered because the higher one goes into fields of light, the greater the speed, and it could be compared to being struck by a bolt of lightning unless the whole of the being is prepared for such transmission. Once this specific degree of radiation is established it becomes a group voltage, and a colour-tone may be sent through the field of transmission and directed to create certain specific effects.

6 September 1954

You have been experimenting with what you call colour-tone and its uses in effecting changes in the earth and within the ethers surrounding it. We shall attempt to give you a definite thought form in regard to the use of so-called colour-tone. You may take it thus:

All is light, light is radiation, radiation becomes colour and/or tone. The two are equivalent. Example: The light descends. It descends in circular forms, from the point from which it is spontaneously projected. It is an intense white light (heat) but as it continues to expand in circumference it becomes slowed down in relative motion and appears to take on both colour and tone; or, more precisely, it radiates as such to the consciousness that comprehends it.

Premise: It must then have a point or apex in degree in order that it may be released in form, or as specific light waves. It must have an objective or there would be no purpose in releasing it. It must manifest according to its nature, which reveals itself according to the degree of receptivity.

Its manifestation as colour and tone carries with it specific degrees of radiance which are related to the qualities of being as understood by the human mind. Therefore, in order to become aware of the qualities inherent within the degree of light so released, man must become conscious of the reason for projecting it upon, through and around the planet earth.

Thought: were man to realize that peace is an inherent quality within the mind of God—that it has colour and tone in balanced degree—that it is being radiated through the ethers by dedicated servers known as light bearers—that it may be absorbed as one would absorb sunlight by receptivity to it—then man would soon end his warring tendencies and become one with the quality of peace in radiation.

16 October 1954

Conflict in the mind of man is followed by conflict in the elements. The etheric envelope of the earth can only be harmonized by an exact degree of radiation from the causal realms, linked with an harmonious vibrational condition as a projection of the consciousness of the man of earth.

You ask, how is the vibrational condition achieved when man is agitated, fearful and insecure?

It cannot be. However, the descending substance (elements) cannot be deterred by the state of consciousness in which man finds himself; and their releases are constant. The colour tone which is their quality of being will eventually do its work.

We spoke of the colour-tone quality of peace, the sustaining power of the blue radiation, but neither the colour-tone nor quality can be effective unless the mind receptive to them harmonizes with them.

30 October 1954

Learn to harmonize all conditions around you by learning to absorb the incoming colour-tone radiations and to release them as a sub-conscious habit. Were children taught the meaning of the colour-tones as they are taught to read, vibrational harmony would be established very quickly.

All ideas come from the Mind of God, or the universal realms of the All-Knowing; therefore man is at liberty to draw upon them at any time, testing and substantiating his findings by manifest evidence.

Our desire is to bring the cosmic or higher dimensional response into form for the use of man on earth in the transitional period which is now a part of his progress. We can do so in several ways, by directing radiations which help to expand and quicken the understanding; by placing on record (as you are now doing) the findings which will help to substantiate that understanding; and by a process of light-descent into the pooled reservoirs so that the solar substance may be drawn upon in time of great need.

After much study it has been revealed that within each colour tone there is a principle of being—a quality which is in essence the very nature of Being.

We have said that BLUE is the foundational substance and that the substance of being reflects the colour blue. The quality of substance is strength, reflected in tone throughout the stratosphere and the etheric light-wave currents surrounding the earth. Each major colour of the spectrum is a reflection of the qualities within ALL-BEING and each is as a lighted lamp to the man of earth so that he may see his way into the vaster expanse of Being and harmonize with it.

The tonal qualities of the spectrum are only vaguely grasped by the human mind. Man feels inharmonious, ill at ease with his surroundings, but blames it on some condition, person or thing. He fails to realize that harmonizing with the etheric light waves would bring him relief and recognition of the potentials within the tonal qualities of being. He has to be taught by absorbing the radiations and becoming aware of the possibilities within them, by carefully prepared instruction as to their use and meaning.

Radiation must be felt before it can be seen: it must be directed into the etheric consciousness before it can be felt. A study of it must be placed on record so that the mind of man may contemplate the written word, thereby confirming that which has reached him through his vibrational response.

12 November 1954

You are to remember that the *all is the one mind* and that the One Mind is *in all, over all and through all.*

Thus whenever a contact is made through deep faith, and in the belief that results will follow, then the being becomes receptive to the channels through which the *one mind* is active, i.e. the initiates. No man comes to know the Father until he has learned to still the being to receptivity to the indwelling Presence. It is through this stillness that he comes to recognize his oneness with the All-Knowing; then no matter how he receives, or through what channels, he is receiving direct from the Mind of God.

I am a pure channel through which the ideas of spirit flow. I can measure my growth by my response to those ideas.

Throughout the ages of the Earth there have always been men who have known the truth, who have had access to the so-called Mysteries, who have been sent to perform a mission among their fellow men, and who have done so through sacrifice and suffering in order that the Light might penetrate the darkness, finally meeting no opposition and thus creating Light paths which could easily be followed by the man of earth. The time is now again ripe for these Light Bearers. The Great Overlighting Ones are carefully preparing the way for the fullness of Light to shine upon the earth. It is only through careful preparation that it may be done, and that man will see himself as the son of God, and therefore be able to create his own kingdom of peace and harmony.

* * * *

Today let us take the colour tone of Yellow. Its meaning to you is joy, freedom, release from burdens, a spontaneous rhythm which is completely relaxing. Can this colour tone be released in great volumes over, into and through the earth planet? Would it be possible for the consciousness of man to receive great quantities of joy, to relax in them as he would in the sunshine of a warm, sandy beach? Think on these things.

20 November 1954

Now, as to the use of solar radiance as we have tested it in our workshops: solar radiation is applicable to all which appears in manifestation, yet is in itself an invisible condition of being, relating to the movement of the Light forces throughout the universe. Thus is it distinguished from what you know as solar substance, which is a vitalizing quality of being, now being released into the earth's ethers for the specific purpose of enhancing and transforming all that pertains to earth manifestation, until a planet becomes enlightened.

We have found our underground dwelling, which has been extended far beyond the knowledge of those by whom we were incarcerated, completely illumined by a bluish quality of light which took on a variety of colourings according to our thoughts, or in response to our spoken word. This seemed proof to us that we were inducing by our thought forms, or by our tone of voice, certain light reflections. These changed only when we changed the principal character of our thought projections.

For example, despair or dark brooding thoughts carry with them heavy greyish black colouring; longing for outside world conditions would bring with them greenish-brown lights which were distracting and very unsettling. Physical conditions of pain or lack of ease would reflect in a sulphurous light which gave off an odour as well as colour.

If the tones of our voices were weak, uncertain, speaking of lack, fear, irresolution, or any quality unlike that represented by faith, the atmosphere around us would produce a kind of singing sound which was extremely irritating, lacking both harmony and rhythm.

27 November 1954

The first results of our findings were negative because we were prepared only for the negative. We worked through many testings and much which was apparently detrimental before we began to be aware of a vast field of exploration which could and did open new vistas of livingness for us.

Our first awareness that we were actually responsible for the conditions in which we found ourselves was when after deep prayer and a united willingness to improve our situation, we found that we were overlighted by a Presence—a very great Presence, full of colour, who began speaking to us. As He spoke we found that we were able to see His radiations; they were brilliant beyond belief, so brilliant that we were unable to face them and knelt in our darkened cave overcome with awe and a premonition that we were entering the Kingdom of Heaven. This belief brought with it the thought that we were about to lay aside our physical bodies, and a great fear came upon us. We begged to be allowed to stay in our world of form, no matter how limited, until we knew more and could be of some use in it. The Presence again came and spoke to us. He said that within each of us was the power to overcome death; that we might dwell in bodies of light and bring that Light to mankind, were we willing to make the sacrifice.

He reminded us that He had gone from the Cross to the tomb where he had lain in darkness deprived of bodily functioning. He then told us that the Spirit, whom He knew to be the Greater Self, spoke to Him and admonished Him, reminding Him that He had cast out devils, healed the sick and restored the blind to sight. Was He then to permit His power to lie dormant because He could not function in a physical form?

His was the great testing, for through the power of the Word He had to reassume the form which had been laid out in so-called death, and prove to the world that this was possible. He began then to use that power, deliberately calling forth the elements which made up the physical body. He knew the power of the Word, but this was His supreme test.

He continued to visit us and to give us details of that supreme experience. We were still afraid to face the Great Master, but with each visit a flood of light filled us, and we were aware that we were seeing in the dark many wonderful colours, that we were hearing tones which awakened the cell life within us to renewal; that we were where we were for a purpose, and until that was fulfilled we could not go.

3 December 1954

It was some time before we could bear the radiance which proceeded from our Beloved. The rhythm was such that we could not rise from our knees, much less face the light that came from Him. But His gentleness and the love that came to us as a living force finally empowered the cell life of the soul-being; and we came to gaze upon His beautiful features and to listen to His voice in the stillness as we visibly expanded under the radiance.

His first instruction to us was that we were there for a specific purpose; that we had been chosen to make this experiment and that He would help us to understand the lives which made this life possible. He explained in simple terms—in our language—that we were to re-attempt what He had accomplished two thousand years ago, so that man might have understanding of the Light and might come to live in it and express himself through it. He told us that His earthly life, as recorded in the New Testament, was to prepare man for this test two thousand years later. He also told us that the New Testament record was incomplete, partial, but that as it stood it had become *The Word* for man through the centuries.

He also told us that He had never left the earth; that His Presence was known of many and He appeared in many places to give help where it was needed, making Himself known to those who were ready to seek Him in form, and by means of His radiation to those who as yet could not see. He told us that through the centuries since His recorded appearance we had served in many capacities, doing His work as it was given us to do; that our testing was a supreme one, for what we were called upon to endure might ultimately destroy the physical body if we failed to perceive that we dwelt in Light no matter how great the darkness of the earth. But He also told us that He could not have come to us had we not been able to accept in faith the radiations preceding His coming; and that now our work would be shown us day by day.

7 January 1955

After our Lord and Master had presented Himself to us many times, and we had become accustomed to His vibrations and to the resulting force, which not only enlightened our cavern, but filled it with such positive radiance that we were transmuted to another plane of activity, we became aware that we were actually bringing into form various manifestations of the healing, restorative powers of such radiance. For instance, one among us had for a long time been the victim of running sores which proved unhealable; but by the visits of the Master, and the resultant penetration of our darkened dwelling with colour-sound vibrations, the sores were healed and the skin became pure and translucent in appearance.

One of us was blinded and sat for days in darkness. His sight was restored, and together we received the baptism of the Holy Spirit which permitted us to see the inner planes and to carry on our work through them. Many were the transformations that took place in mind and body. Our emotional life was now stabilized, and we were able to dwell in the inner kingdoms without struggle, bringing forth our findings with clarity and ease.

In time we discovered how to make use of the solar substances and were permitted to experiment in fields hitherto unknown to us. We found that bird life responded very quickly, being vibrantly in rhythm. Birds were trained to become responsive to our tests. Some became messengers carrying the radiance to our comrades who were imprisoned above ground. Others were sent on errands of mercy to far distances, taking with them the healing light.

We were shown great fields of dwarfed and stunted trees, and planes where nothing of life seemed to be maintained. We tested the solar substance with great care, and found response in full grown verdant trees, grass, flowers and vegetation hitherto unknown to us. These testing grounds of the earth plane may be uncovered soon, so that the eyes of man may see the transformation.

4 February 1955

Our response elucidated the power of the colour-sound radiations communicated by the Holy Presence, and their effect upon us and upon our surroundings. This became increasingly evident as we dwelt upon the qualities within them and learned that in so doing they not only increased our will to do and to be, but also suggested to us the possibilities of manifestation in form. We thus became aware of our own Indwelling Presence, of the unlimited potential within, and the possibilities of creating a totally new world of form.

This was a slow process, one in which we could not measure time; but before we could commit our minds to the truth that man is a creator of his own world, we had first to eliminate from consciousness all preconceived ideas; all that held us to the pattern of the man of the world, all that bound us to the negative; for only the positive would respond to tonal qualities.

We dwelt in long silences, unbroken by the sound of our voices; then again we would be impelled to speak the Creative Word, aligning ourselves with its radiations. Gradually we began to see, as it came from the void, the beginning of the *word* as it began to manifest in form. We beheld the shape of the idea, its colouring, the various shadings as the radiations were used to form the pattern. We saw it as though in embryo, a faint, but nevertheless distinct impression of our thought forms as they were infused with the power of Light. The radiations then began to increase in brillance and slowly we perceived that we were dealing with the actual substance of being, unformed, undifferentiated, lending itself in increasing fullness to our thought forms. We then were able to see the necessity for the long ordeal of erasing all that was unlike the pure essence of the solar substance. It could only be conceived when met on its own level of being. It became malleable and responsive to thought only when that thought equalized with its inherent awareness of pure being. We could not use it to create our desires in form, unless those desires were as clear and pure in essence as were the radiations from which they came.

It was a long, laborious task to raise our minds to the same degree of radiation. It meant constant watchfulness of every vibration sent forth. The enemy was ever with us, injecting the poison of misconception, using every allure of the flesh to conquer the man of Spirit. But when we found the opposing forces too intense, we dwelt upon the Love of God, as manifest through His Messengers throughout the ages known to man. Also, we came to meet these great Masters on their own level of being. We came to know that we were earth beings because we had so chosen, but that we might meet and mingle with beings of other planets, learning from them again, so it seemed, the truths which were a part of our inner awareness, but dulled by our life in physical form. Practice of the Presence of the Holy Ones is a necessity, for through them one learns to vibrate in harmony with the celestial radiations.

11 February 1955

Greetings to our beloved workers in the Light, who accept without witnessing, believe without proof.

To recapitulate: We discovered that our colour radiations were in direct relation to our state of consciousness. If it was low, then the vibrational colours were dark and gloomy. We discovered that we could bring about glorious colours in our darkened world by the power of thought. We discovered that our bodies were healed by the radiation of Light in colour and tone, as directed to us by our Beloved. We discovered that we could manifest from the substance of being through the tonal qualities of the radiations that which was necessary to our well being. Thus we were prepared to begin to experiment with the use of substance in undifferentiated form. Pure substance of being acted upon by pure thought became a work of art, a curative essence. The producer of forms in nature (such as flowers and trees); increased and deepened the colour tones and formed many shades not as yet known to man.

We were years, as man counts time, experimenting with the radiations until we became sure that we were dealing with a substance which had endlesss powers or potentials of manifestation. Everywhere the substance was available to the man who was willing to reach into the higher dimensions and accept in faith what he found.

As this substance began to envelop us in our surroundings, we found that we were out of body form as often as we were in it. We became able effortlessly to transcend the body, returning to it when the need was to keep our earth habitation. Thus we began our life of experimentation by "going abroad". We conducted, along with our Brothers of Light on other planets, the experiments which are to be used by earth man when he is ready to receive them.

A specific discovery is that peace has a colour-tone the harmony of which, if sounded by man universally, would instantly restore him to that condition upon the earth. It has to do with the forces of nature as well as with the mental attitude of man, but has largely to do with his faith in the God of his nature.

Dwell upon this.

18 February 1955

We learned by our mistakes, by our errors in judgment, by our lack of discrimination. In other words, we learned our lessons in experience just as all men must learn them. But our sense of values deepened with the experiments made.

We were dealing with universal substance, with the basic reality of Being, therefore, though we might err in our understanding or approach to its use, it of itself was eternal—the life-giving quality; that upon which we could draw and did draw for our very existence in a darkened cave away from the walks of men, and as restricted as living can be.

We understood that the solar radiation had a rhythmic movement; that within its movements were contained colour and tone that might be heard by the ear finely attuned to the higher dimensions. We also understood that if we could make man aware of this condition of being, he would never return to his present manner of life. We were faced, therefore, with the necessity not only of continuing our experiments, but of finding a way to make them known to man on the subjective planes, so that he might discover for himself that which we knew to be the very law and foundation of his being, and thereafter would begin to manifest the results of such knowledge. Just as naturally as he ate, breathed and slept, he would create from the pure substance of being the ideas which through his creative ability he could bring into manifestation.

Long arduous days and nights were spent in theorizing over how we might be able to bring to the consciousness of man knowledge now needful for his survival upon the planet on which he finds himself. The solution seems to lie within the fact that we as men of earth, though far removed from its activities, had become aware of this great truth and by our daily efforts were able to bring forth results which were astounding to us and which would revolutionize the consciousness of man.

Our contacts with beings of other planets made it clear to us that we could learn from them how they had achieved such results; how they applied what they knew as reality to their objective life; how watchful they must be in so doing, for while they were evolved far beyond the awareness of the earth man, yet they too had their problems, among them the restoration of the Solar Being as it left the earth plane existence and came to their planet, and/or planets, for recuperation and for teaching. Thus we discovered that many had the solar substance injection before returning to earth to help their fellow man, but that the *time is now for all men of earth to become aware of the potentiality of their being, before earth is swept away from him.*

25 February 1955

Colour and tone, as you have been told, are the direct results of the vibration of Light, i.e. radiation. Solar radiation is the power within the vibrations. Colour and tone are the concommitants of such radiation. As they increase in speed, or in high dimensional quality, they become more vibrant and therefore more brilliant. They are then unrecognizable to the man whose consciousness is not in tune with the higher vibrations. Were they to be seen they would appear only as brilliant white light, which would be unbearable in its intensity.

Solar radiation, therefore, must be relayed to the man of earth in a degree which will not prove injurious to him. It must also be radiated in such a manner that resistance is not set up to it, which could easily be the result of a higher degree of radiation than his bodies, physical, mental or emotional, can sustain. It is therefore a very delicate manipulation to learn how to use and to earn the right to use the solar radiations; to interpret them as to their tonal qualities, and to relay them into the mind of man through prepared channels.

Now we through receptivity and daily experiment have tested the degree which we could tolerate and its effect upon the substance around us. We have noted the response in the physical reaction of our bodies, in the skin tones, hair and eyes. We in fact have re-made our physical bodies; but we have also had to consider the effect upon our emotional and mental vehicles. These have been accelerated far beyond their normal scope and an adjustment to each degree of infiltration has to be made.

Thus it is that a specific degree of radiation is now being injected into man. Before earth can change and bear good fruits, his entire consciousness must be raised to carry the degree of light which will make it possible. No longer must he prepare for death by destructive weapons; he must be prepared to realize that his very thought forces carry destruction or its opposite. Bear the thought in mind *that man creates either his good or his evil by the power of his thought.*

4 March 1955

We discovered that the essence or substance of being is ever present within the radiations. As we came to use them we could do many things of which we were not previously capable. The very tones of the vibrations were capable of creating physical ease, calmness of approach and serenity of mind. We learned to attune ourselves to a delicate beauty of sound within the finer vibrations. We learned also to make ourselves so receptive to the light waves as they came to us that we could mingle with them and become one with their radiations.

Thus while we were attempting to record the results of our findings we became what you might call etherealized. Our bodies were refined to a pure channel for the stream of light now being transmitted to us. Our coarse daily diet merely sufficed to maintain life, but we came to know that we needed very little food in order to keep our bodies strong, fine and clean. We were at all times absorbing the rarefied essence of the true quality of being. Our auras took on tremendously brilliant colourings, and with such transformation came the ability to translate our consciousness to a place where we could unite with those who were receiving the higher instructions.

11 March 1955

In all our work we acknowledged the Presence of the Christ in our midst. We knew that without His radiations nothing was possible to us, and with them "*all things are possible*". His coming was our signal to work, to study, to test through experiment as did He when living among men in the physical form. But we also knew that by giving recognition to His radiations they became a part of us and we were uplifted in mind, healed in body and made receptive in heart to the greater teachings. We knew that man must first learn to live with his fellow men before he can become aware that he is a spiritual being and can wield the Light. *The Light in itself is an impersonal force and may be wielded as a destructive weapon as well as one which brings forth forbearance, faith and hope to mankind.*

We therefore learned to live with each other, not without difficulty under such conditions. This was a test of our ability to mingle our radiations, to love, to serve and to manifest patience. After many tests we became finally as one man, each acting according to his individual pattern or mould. No two men are alike, each is an individual in God's sight, as are the finger prints. Each must learn his lessons in his own way, but in learning them come to the full realization that he is one with the great all-knowing, all-seeing Presence, and can never be separate from any of its manifestations. "Do unto other as ye would be done by"; "Love thy neighbour as thyself" became our watchwords.

Our thought for today: *love one another so that you may fully experience the harmony of the vibrations of light.*

25 March 1955

So deeply have we gone into the pain that makes for pure manifestation of the Christ Love, that we feel the experience of each individual. Nothing is achieved in expression of the Love without pain, patience and perseverance. Out of the darkness comes the light, and man cannot give full recognition to the Light until he has dwelt in darkness. After repeated tests over many years we came to know that the finest, most subtle shadings must be used if we were to achieve harmony; and if we could not achieve harmony, how then could we expect to transmit our radiations for the good of all men? Then came a time when we found a subtle blending of forces which would ease tension, dissolve fear, and render the consciousness receptive to the great impersonal love which is the atmosphere we breathe. Mother of pearl, translucently beautiful, with many fine irradiations of the qualities of love, could best reach the consciousness of man. *Love is the very substance of being, the foundation of life itself and the harmony of all spheres in expression.*

8 April 1955

The whole body of man, physical, emotional and mental, is composed of very fine radiations. That he is unaware of this makes it no less true. The cell life is in a constant state of transmutation in response to such radiations, and man's thought processes determine what he becomes, when he has resolved to become a being of light who can make or remake his manifest form according to his desires. Our desire was, after receiving the Presence and becoming aware of His mission, to project radiant bodies which would in turn become servers or saviours of mankind. We made many tests throughout years of measured time, to discover how we could manifest in form in the very heart of the earth, delivering it from its condensed state of consciousness and also delivering man from bondage to that heavy condensation. We knew it to be a matter of vibration, a quality of irradiation which would stimulate the use of accelerated currents of light. But how to enter the earth and project the necessary accelerated currents?

We tested by digging deep in our own caves and going in body form to animate the life of the earth. This produced some response but was actually little more than a man who digs for coal or other minerals may do. We knew then that we ourselves must be so transformed that the earth would open to receive us. We began our translation into the finer elements by refraining from the coarse food set before us. We began to use the "Manna from Heaven", or the etherealized substance. We partook only of this, finding consolation in the Presence, who seemed to be always available. We used the colour tone radiations as they had been presented to us, and they became a part of us. We then seemed to go into deep trance, where we beheld the physical body as light and light only. We were shown the heart of the earth opening to us as the womb of a mother open to receive the seed. We felt ourselves to be a unit enfolded within the earth and it became one with us.

Then only did we feel the transformation of the higher voltage to that of the lesser, and the transition begin to take place.

Our records do not show the length of time, but we became indeed earth beings, partaking of the substance of Mother Nature.

22 April 1955

Once we were within the bowels of the earth we found that they were capable of expansion, of great resilience which manifested in the spreading of the particles of substance composing what we call earth. It is dense only as the mind of man beholds it. But when awareness has been elevated to the recognition of light particles, and their relationship to matter in vibrational expression, then density is replaced by the movement of the particles according to the light inplayed upon them in sufficient degree to accelerate them. Matter as such is merely condensation of the light particles. It takes form according to the pattern set by man. He is and always has been the creator of that upon which he lives. If he beholds it as dense, difficult, destructive, subject to the elements, or in whatsoever way he perceives its substance, then it become what he beholds. We found the earth expanding to our radiations. It spread into fine irridescent particles and within them we were able to see jewels of rare beauty and incomparable worth.

We do not mean to infer that the average man might go into the bowels of the earth and demand of it that it give forth rare jewels or minerals which would create riches for him alone. But when he is prepared to translate his body into one of Light, and radiate that light into the densities of matter, he will find that it is subject to the form he wishes to give it.

10 June 1955

Today we would like to give you a brief summary so that you will again find the rhythm of our resonse and be able to take our findings literally. As we have told you, we are conscious ever of being in the *Great Presence.* We abide in his radiations in full consciousness that they are the redeeming force. They appear to us in many variations of the basic colours, and as we see them depicted in various forms and phases, we find the qualities of being clearly assembled for our preview. You would like a further explanation of that statement. It is that as we invoke a beam or degree of radiation, it is displayed for us in its varied and numerous shades, which means its various effects when translated into form. We find many manifestations not as yet visible to the eye of man, yet ready for him when he is ready to make them real. This accounts for the many and brilliant colourings now visible in your skies, for as the radiations go forth into the ethers they become a part of your atmosphere and are absorbed by all who are responsive to them.

The next step is for man to realize that such radiations are actually a part of his being, and definitely related to his permanence upon the earth. This means that as he absorbs them, he relates himself, i.e. his consciousness, to the ray from which they are transmitted, and in due time finds consciousness expanding to admit the peculiar and transcendent qualities of that ray. There are seven major rays which individualize seven basic qualities of being. Peace has a strong, harmonious beam reflecting the light in many variations, but always in the harmony which we see reflected in nature; in the same way the other primal rays have their own distinct colour connotations. There are many, each nuance or shading reflecting to a minute degree a certain aspect of the quality of being dominant within it. Peace in its fullest connotation is harmony in relation to all forms of manifestation. Music (true music) is a great purveyor of the radiations known as peace. Colour as transmitted through spiritual channels is another positive purveyor of this quality. Peace is always existent, always in exact rhythmic response to the realms in which it is known and accepted. The mind of man must be capable of acceleration to that degree, and as it is stepped up by the opening of the heart centre, *peace* becomes an accepted condition of being. It is thus that we behold it, but we could not do this until our whole being was aligned with the radiations and we were clear, pure channels for it.

17 June 1955

Our experiments were carried out because of and with the enhancement of the great overlighting radiations. As these came to us in greater magnitude we were able to interpret more fully the meaning of the qualities within the rays thus displayed.

Today we should like to present for your enlightenment an understanding of the *Ray of Love*. Love has many qualities and many underlying aspects. We feel love and see its reflection in a variety of forms. But until a deep study has been made of the radiation, as for instance from the man Jesus, one has a very passive and incomplete idea of its meaning. Love in its basic colour radiation is a rose-pink of an indescribable hue and an unforgettable fragrance. It is beyond our words to give you the inner meaning of this basic quality of being. It is the essence of all manifestation, and is inbreathed with the solar breath wherever a man is receptive. Once his aura is prepared to receive and give it forth, the hues deepen and change with the character of the man's thoughts and with the manifestation of his aura. Love, therefore, may have many related shades from the pale, pearly pink of an embryo dawn to deep rose red. None of the colours which you see upon or within the earth's reflection even begin to depict those reflected from the Great Ones whose purpose it is to bring them to men of earth. The ray of Love is the greatest because it has the essence of all things within it, and from it all things are madc. Man gains much hy practising this quality of being in relation to his world; but not until the manifestation through Christ's auric being could he begin to know that Love is the whole of life, and that to become one with it is to become a being of such splendour that manifestation on any plane of being is possible and may be instantaneous. The Brotherhood of light is composed of those who seek to serve the Christ Light, no matter how devious the way or how great the difficulties encountered. This we discovered only after we had beheld the Great Presence and felt His enlightening radiations. The desire or the need for Him invokes His Presence, and His Presence evokes the radiations which become the means of enlightening the world.

24 June 1955

We should like to begin again to describe to you our discovery that we could enter the bowels of the earth in body form, not of course our concrete or physical body but its Light replica. We appeared to one another to be composed of positive radiation, which gave off both colour and tone, and through which the cell life could be seen. We were consciously aware that we were acting as transformers, carrying our currents into the earth and by means of them quickening to life what had been dense material. Night after night as we progressed in our transmission of the radiations and in the transforming, transmitting capacity, we became aware that many changes were taking place. Hard mineral surfaces changed to translucent irridescence, almost blinding in their colour-tone qualities. Clay dissolved into a finer essence and seemed to be used as a means of sustaining us while we made our experiments. We found that vegetation could be transformed into instantaneous growth and could be taken in liquid form that would sustain life for long periods without the necessity of taking in the coarser foods. This experiment was made in our normal physical forms, thus lessening our desire for the extremely coarse fare provided for us. We tested all our findings in the laboratory of our daily lives. We had to be convinced that we were not partaking of an illusory or dream life, but that what we found in our nightly pilgrimages into the earth could be used in the daily life of man, thus helping to transmute his material being into one of stronger, more penetrative form.

Whatever we take into our bodies, mind or emotional being, is used either to create density, a slowing down process, or to elevate our cell life and thus to enlighten and increase our powers.

1 July 1955

Our experiments within the earth's surface led us to believe that the fine vibrations which we carried with us in order to penetrate the denser substance, were particles of light radiance or solar substance. In other words, they accelerated to a degree capable of penetrating denser fields, and were also capable of transmuting and transforming as they were transmitted. How they came to be in the exact degree necessary for this purpose was for us to find out. Our first experiments were rough, having to do largely with the need for self preservation; then as we came to feel more at ease within our field we came to realize that had we not been able to assume the auric vehicles we could not possibly have attempted such experiments. We came to see and study our auric transmissions, finding within them the subtle radiations which, for instance, would cut through dense matter, would open channels for distribution of colour-tone.

There seemed at first to be a cutting sensation, but as the harmony was established this reaction disappeared and instead we found our vehicles manifesting much as they might above ground, in the air, or elsewhere. We were light bodies of vivid colour and extraordinarily musical tones. We knew no discomfort, but rather felt a harmonious rhythmic state of being which filled us with elation. We found that the inner earth had an especially fluidic response, as though having so long contained its own vibrations it was joyous and released to respond to the radiatons from above; that having found their degree of radiation we could blend ours with it in a harmonious, creative awakening of the powers within all manifestation.

7 July 1955

All mineral content is being changed by the radiations inplayed, and as men begin to investigate they will find rare combinations which they will undoubtedly conclude is a new species. We have found all dense matter susceptible to the changing vibrations and capable of being transmuted into finer substance thereby. The diamond is a highly charged emanation of pure white light, converted into crystalline form by the action of the earth emanations. Those we found could be changed so that the content of the diamond crystal could become soluble, a stream of brilliant blue and white colouring. We experimented also with other jewel-like manifestations and found that they might be converted into streams of pure energy which would in turn make it possible to create higher forms of life. By "higher forms" we mean those capable of transmitting and transmuting energies.

It slowly dawned upon our consciousness that our radiations and/or vibrations were being used to break up the heavy dense substances of which the earth is composed, to enlighten them, freeing them from the chemical content which limited or restricted the basic forms. As we tested we found—after many experiments—that we were creating pure substance out of dense matter, and therefore our conclusion must be that all matter is in essence pure substance, capable of reduction to its rarefied form. This means that the earth could respond to the descending energies and thereby be transformed. Then it was that we began to make our formulae or picture projections if you will. We saw that energy acting upon matter created form; or changed, renewed and recreated old form. Having made this discovery in regard to the earth content, we recognized that we must now build new thought forms by means of which the substance might give forth new forms of life, i.e. a tree might still be a tree, yet become so animated with the life-giving radiations that it would be capable of manifesting in a much higher vibration, or a much more sentient way.

23 July 1955

It was some time before we came to understand that we were dealing in *substance*; that it not only was that of which we were composed but in its higher, more accelerated, form was the Light that inspired the creation of which it was the form. This meant, of course, that *all is Light* and that it was the Light acting upon itself in the degree of its radiation which caused the manifestation in form. This again related to colour and tone. At specific degrees of radiation the Light took on myriad colourings and each one of these had a specific tone or quality which could be heard, not of course by the mortal ear whose response to sound is very low, but which in the higher octaves was a symphony in colour-tone. This led to the premise that Light must be acted upon before it becomes substance and takes form. Then if all is Light how could it be acted upon by something other than itself?

Light began to relate itself to substance and substance to form according to a tremendous *over-all power* which had a plan, and out of which came the Universes of Light and by means of which they were sustained in order and in form. We could not give recognition to the magnitude of this Over-Soul or All-Knowing Power other than to call it God. This we had to accept as the foundation upon which all things are created, and from which all that is came into being. But in our efforts to follow the relationship of Light to creation we came to know that a specific of the All-Knowing Power was inherent in us; and that as we gave recognition to it, it grew and expanded into a greater force; and through that we came to develop our theories and make our tests. If that Light could penetrate the dense conditions of the earth's substance, refining them until they became part of our awareness, and we could enter that substance in our higher vibrational bodies, then there could be no absence of light anywhere; it is simply a matter of acceptance of the degree by the consciousness of man. We accepted that "all things were possible" to us because it was a promise made by the Master Who came to teach us the qualities of the radiations; that whatever man believed in became possible to him.

5 August 1955

We became aware as we continued our tests that certain colours had definite form, or rather could be used according to their qualities so as to manifest form; the colour *yellow*, for instance, which to you means freedom, joy, relief from tension. This is an out-giving quality of being. As we experimented in the transmission of those qualities within the depths of the earth itself, we found the denser vibrations responding and a golden glow as of filtered sunshine appearing throughout the heavy, dense material form. It seemed to radiate through us, into and around us, breaking up density into fine particles. As these were broken a misty substance appeared which would take form according to the thoughts directed towards it. We experimented by creating beautiful, jewel-like flowers. In them we could see any colour we desired, but we could not make them without the use of the freeing, releasing, transmuting quality which in its essence is Yellow. This was an illuminating process. We took yellow then *as a basic, freeing or transforming phase of the solar substance.*

13 August 1955

But we had many other tonal qualities to appraise, analyse and test. That with which we had to mingle our radiations in order to make our tests was heavy and dense, inert. In other words our experiments were actually making the earth come alive. We wish to make ourselves very clear on this: *we are by no means without physical bodies.* We use them wherever it is necessary to do so, just as does every other man in physical manifestation. But we have come to know that such bodies may be separate and apart from our actual livingness, and we may accelerate our spiritual or solar bodies to the point where they may go anywhere we wish them to go. Until man as a whole has come to accept this as the truth of his being, it is not likely that he will accept the truth that we can actually become a part of the earth by desiring so to do.

We continued our experiments to the point where we proved that the colour-tone known as yellow—yet containing many other variations of that principle—was actually the transforming agent in relation to denser vibrations. We compared it with sunlight acting upon plant life, with the richness of newly minted gold, with as many of the forms of its manifestation as we could collect.

19 August 1955

We continued to record our experiences so that they might become real to the mind of man. Nothing becomes real to him until he has proved it for himself. His very life upon the earth is a process of experiment. As he progresses in the recognition of the possibilities within the mind he becomes increasingly aware of the possibilities within his livingness. It was to this truth that we were led by our experiments within the earth. We came to make them only when we perceived that it was possible for us to detach ourselves from the physical, but that in order to do so we had to build for ourselves dynamic light bodies. Our belief is that a Light Body must be earned. It is not awarded to an individual just by his belief in being good; he must learn to become dynamically conscious of the Light, to wield it in the service of others; *to be conscious of the powers contained within such a body and to be aware that if misused it will act as a destructive agency.*

We based our desire to learn upon the principles set forth in the teachings of Jesus, Who reflected the qualities of the Christed Being so that they came to be accepted by countless thousands. He, the Master, came to us after we had begun our search and were dedicated to the belief that these principles alone could save us. That He has appeared to many others after the search had begun is also true. We began to study His radiations, and as we continued we found within them living qualities which we too might manifest. Colour and tone were shown us in form and as we made them ours we became that form. Slowly the veil was lifted and we became aware that matter was only a denser form of the vibrations of Light. That all was the one substance, the eternal radiation of the One Light, but that the degree of its radiation was the answer to the multiplicity of form.

We believe that we were chosen to make the experiment within the densest form in order to prove to man the possibilities within the Light Body. But first of all we had to know of what the Light Body consisted. How could it maintain form independent of the physical body? How did it do so, and for what purpose? If it then were possible to have such magnificent bodies based on radiation, why the physical and its recurrent sufferings? Our enforced confinement and limitation as to food helped us in rejecting the physical demands, but we had to accept our physical bodies as a very real part of our being and learn to use them in accordance with the principles of the body of Light. They could not be cast aside because it was through them that the great manifestation of the powers within the Body of Light must be made.

10 September 1955

We are ready now to begin the presentation of our findings as they relate to tone as well as to colour. By tone we mean the reflection of the colour upon the etheric Light-waves. It does have harmonious vibrations which can be heard by the attuned ear. Frequently in our work within the earth we caught these vibrations and became so one with them that the tone was both audible and visible.

Our first experiments were largely in the field of transmutation. We watched the effect of the radiations upon what is called matter and watched it dissolve into tiny particles of irridescent substance. It appeared to break and re-form into a fine, mistlike quality which much later became visible to our eyes as an infinite variety of colour. We studied this until we became aware that it was the power of our own thoughts which caused this substance to take form, and that as it did so in varying shades and hues we could hear these delicate, imperceptible wave lengths as they moved from one form to another.

As we continued our investigation along these lines we became aware that we were living in a world of wondrous harmony. Music was everywhere around us, and we began to be able to associate it with the various colour forms. If we desired the beauty of flowers, we had but to think the thought of a rose, a violet, or whatever form we desired. It would appear in fragrant beauty beyond description and the musical vibrations accompanying it would be those of utter harmony. We made a test on the thought of jewels, of crystal, of many other forms in substance, and always a transformation would take place and we would begin to hear celestial music.

7 October 1955

We have been defining for you the fundamentals of the approaching change in the general consciousness and in the material aspects of man's earth living as the perceptive fields of consciousness become more developed and as you prepare to enter realms of greater radiation. Men will in time bear the Light Bodies, which is their solar radiation, upon the earth. Animal consciousness will be elevated. The very contents of the earth itself will change. Man will have to learn to live in such a world and produce for himself that which he needs; he will have an entirely different environment and an entirely different attitude towards it.

Our findings, we believe, are applicable to the conditions in which mankind now finds himself. The attempt to make peace while still preparing for war obviously has no foundation of reality. The principal question which man now must ask himself is, how do I create peace? The answer is simple, but until his consciousness appropriates the qualities of peace, there will continue to be wars and strife in every department of his living. Peace is a quality of being which means harmonizing with Divine Law. Perhaps we can state it more plainly: *that harmony exists as reality in the upper levels of consciousness and man must reach those levels by means of his thought processes before he can experience harmony and manifest peace as a result.*

Peace then is a vibrational state of being. It has colour tone, rhythm and balance. It has knowledge of itself as a quality of being and from it all harmonies proceed.

We must come to the conclusion that there are two classes of men, those who accept and will the good of all, and those who refuse to give recognition to the spiritual radiations and deliberately choose to dwell in darkness, living for the self as opposed to the One Great Self of All Being. There are many in between those two states of consciousness who might be swayed either way, but in reality there are two major camps arrayed for the final battle of the earth—that of light and darkness. Man has free will, he can choose the side upon which he is to stand. But he cannot have peace until he has filled his earth with light and until all men walk in light in full recognition of its harmonies.

17 October 1955

The time is *now* upon the earth when great changes must come in response to the descent of Light, and there is no time but *now* for man to come to an understanding of his soul powers. They alone can save him from the result of the misuse of such powers. Full recognition must be given to the Light, and to its meaning in relation to the Earth, to its peoples and to the forces which either unite or divide them. There is a simple and reasonable way for man to contact his good, and to make use of it. This way was presented by the Master Jesus, and is still being shown through every available avenue by those who serve Him. The Light descends to illumine the consciousness, but it can only descend through evocation and invocation. It exists and contains within itself all the great livingness displayed by Jesus and expressed through His so-called miracles. But it exists only to the degree the individual consciousness has been able to conceive of it or has hitherto existed only to that degree. The Earth is Mine and I shall come to take it is the promise of the Holy One, *and now is the appointed time.*

21 October 1955

We have spoken about the approach of mankind to the new era, the expanded consciousness. Our mission is largely to create for man channels by means of which he may make that approach. This is reflected through many channels, some as yet little known but which will have their full effect as the consciousness becomes receptive. The harmonizing use of colour tone is one of these. Soul-conscious awareness means that in the upper levels man expresses that which he is as yet unable to grasp in his mind processes as they apply to his physical living. Man has a higher mental body, which is known as his "Solar Being". He has also a physical and emotional body which responds to the higher mental at times, though only very rarely in an incarnation. In other cases a contact is established which permits the individual to carry out impressions given him by the soul or Solar Being. He helps to strengthen the link between the two expressions.

28 October 1955

We have given you our reactions to a few of the major colours of the spectrum:

(1) We know a specific shade of Blue to be very sustaining. We had evidence of this and came to feel an inner strength as the result of reflection upon that tone or colour.

(2) No activity took place other than a receptive, concentrated conscious effort to know why we responded thus to a particular colour or tone. It meant the use of our higher mental faculties, specifically that of concentration and meditation. Every quality of being has a vibrational harmony, or an attunement with all radiation, which sets up a specific in movement throughout the etheric body of the earth. Therefore, if an individual responds harmoniously to a colour-tone he is at one with its vibrations and they may be used to change his physical vehicles, adapted to the higher radiations; and also to alter his emotional response because of his vibrational alignment with their harmonies; and to expand his mental powers through the impact of the energies contained within the specific of vibrational radiation.

4 November 1955

It is now necessary for man to accept that he is a being capable of super-conscious or supernatural awareness. His denial of this truth will only place him beyond the point where help may be given him. When he accepts his God-given potentials he has then become receptive to the qualities inherent within them and is ready to change his vibrational response to the upper levels of being. How is this done? By becoming responsive to the elements contained within the radiation of light. The Light descends as it is invoked by man's acknowledgment of it and his receptivity to it. He may invoke it through prayer or supplication to the

Supreme Light, the God whom he has been taught to worship. In this way he comes slowly to an awareness of the greater Light of which he is a part. He may invoke this radiation by a process which is deep within his soul and which causes him unconsciously to vibrate, or harmonize, with the qualities emanating from the Supreme Life. The elements contained within the radiation of the Light are imperceptible to the eye of man. True he sees colour in the forms of nature, hears purity of tone in muscial compositions, and is uplifted to the degree that he is responsive to them But he does not know that both are the result of the reflection of the harmonies of being on an octave higher than that to which his present consciousness has reached. There have been individuals in every age who have been aware of the Divine Elements, and have given to man their interpretation of them in the arts. But their true inspiration is not known.

11 November 1955

In order to begin to live on the plane of higher mental response, man must believe that such a condition of being is possible. Man for the most part believes in a Divine Presence, one that rules over him in great wisdom and great power. But he is not as yet ready to accept that this Divine Presence is within his self, and may be reached by searching deeply within the planes of his being to find the good for which he longs.

We were exactly at this point in experience when we were incarcerated and for the most part entombed within the earth itself. We believed in a God but a God afar off, one who might or might not listen to our pleas for relief from the horrors of our incarceration. It was not until we had begun to believe in the manifestation of the Divine Powers that we came to see "*all things are possible unto him who believes*".

It was then that we began our testings of the powers of Light as it irradiated our darkened chambers, appeared to us in colour-tone and form; became as it were our Saviour, offering redemption from the confines of our prison walls, but by a means we had never before dreamed of and which could only be tested as reality according to our belief in such means. The radiation brought its own enlightenment. We were then touching higher mental levels sufficiently to begin to experiment with the colour tones as they came to us. We perceived that they uplifted the consciousness, causing physical changes as well. We then carried our experiments further and became conscious that we could transmute and transform our vehicles of manifestation until they became light enough to penetrate even the denser portions of the earth. We had thus found a common meeting ground with the dense particles composing the earth matter and could amalgamate with them, not as physical beings but in our higher mental capacity as beings of Light. How had we done so? By accepting the fact of the colour-tone harmonies, by making them a part of us, by concentrating upon their powers until they became real to us, and then by putting them into action.

The foregoing is a formula for the redemption of the consciousness of man if he will but use it.

18 November 1955

What man does not accept as his reality he cannot know. We discovered that the Light undifferentiated and unformed is the Solar Substance or the sustaining force from which comes all manifestation; that the principle qualities of Being are inherent within the *Light.* That the degree of its manifestation, i.e. radiation, is based upon the degree of its acceptance, or the channelling powers of the consciousness using it; that nature forces are responsive, each according to its degree of receptivity. For example: a tree reflects the quality of strength according to its acceptance of *Solar Substance* as to quantity, aspires to become a tree and unconsciously uses a substance-making quality of "treeness".

We discovered also that the qualities of pure Being, or undifferentiated substance, are inherent within the mind of man; that as he aspires to them in his consciousness they appear as the Powers inherent within the Godhead. The Spirit within him knows and acknowledges the qualities which are in truth the principles of Being. As he applies himself to the acceptance of his spiritual qualities, to that degree they become manifest in form for his use. To dwell upon the qualities of love, wisdom, faith, peace, purity, justice and freedom, is to become one with their radiations, each of which has a specific colour and tone, and to achieve harmony with them. The present age of manifestation is one in which man must find himself as a being of Light; he must use the qualities inherent within to build for himself an enduring world, one in which he may manifest in harmony with the laws of the universe, and thus preserve for himself a continuous form and place of manifestation.

25 November 1955

Having progressed to the point where we accepted the radiations as the qualities of being, and tested their potentials as colour-tone, we became aware of specific changes within our own physical, emotional and mental reflections. We became aware of increasing strength, of dynamic powers which seemed to sustain while they irradiated the mind forces, and of a perception of pure Being within our auric reflection. Physically we seemed to become much lighter; much more easily movable, requiring less food because we were apparently absorbing sustenance from the Solar Substance. It was not until we had reached a high degree of radiation that we became aware that such changes were taking place, and not until we noticed an effulgent blue aura—or etheric transmitting force—around one another that we came to know what we had achieved. We then came to acknowledge that we had, by our many testings and experiments within the qualities of the radiation, become capable of wielding the forces of Light within and from our own centre of being. We began to direct them into the cave-like surroundings which was our place of abode. We literally projected beams of powerful electric blue into the earth walls. To our amazement we found the earth responding, becoming resilient, malleable and dissolving into sparkling particles of light before our very eyes. The next step was to discover why this was possible and how our knowledge could be used. The evidence was before us that man must come to change his consciousness of the earth upon which he dwells in order to accept the degree of light or solar substance which is now being projected into his ethers.

2 December 1955

Our fourth stage followed as the direct result of our discovery that we might project a certain specific colour-tone into dense material and receive positive results therefrom. The test colour-tone, Electric Blue, or Blue Green is of a dynamic quality of being, highly energized and capable of projection when the transmitting channel is on the exact wave-length or vibrational response with it. The form or shape in which it is to be projected must be clearly visualized and held at the same degree of radiation as the wave-length. The projective powers must come from within the solar forces of the being projecting them, and must be directed with force and sufficient powers of intuition to envisage a result. The walls of solid matter may be broken down in this manner, but the transmitting instruments must be capable of entering the denser substance in their Light vehicles or auric being in order to create the form desired. This method of entering the earth substance is now possible, but further experiment must be made. It is, therefore, our premise that the earth itself is soluble, taking any form which may be projected under a given set of circumstances. The magnetic drawing of the earth's substance by means of a specific degree of radiation is possible, and preliminary to the recreation of the planet upon which men have their being.

3 December 1955

The very fact of recording gives substance to what is recorded and sends it forth into the ethers to become reality. Our findings carry within them a concept of being new to the man of earth, yet as limitless as the Universe of Light. They are both fundamental and factual. They have been proven through experiment in experience. They can and will save a planet if accepted as real.

9 December 1955

Our fifth experiment dealt with the potentials inherent within the basic colour-tone and the degree of radiation necessary for its projection in order to bring about an alteration in the physical structure of man. This seemed to us to be the next step. We were conscious of being radically changed in our physical bodies; hence we knew that they must reflect a much more vital auric transmission than men of earth as a whole were capable of reflecting. We also knew that the chemicals within the body material were changed, and in some cases intensified to such a degree that we were uncomfortable in anything but the rarefied atmosphere of the upper reaches of consciousness. When called upon to work at hard labour we were capable of doing so without experiencing any strain or disease. But we were unable to adjust our forces to the limitations which surrounded us. This meant that they must expand if we were to live in confinement and carry on our mission of transmitting the radiations into the earth itself.

We then began our tests of the colour-tone which would alleviate the upsurge of power and strength which we knew that we were drawing from the earth itself; and which we also knew was incoming on waves of Solar Radiance which would stimulate us beyond the point where we might be contained in either our limited environment or our physical bodies. We believed the teachings of the Master Jesus to be that man must build anew his body form, must be able to inhabit it and live upon his earth whilst making contacts with those who have reached the higher levels, transmitting from them to the man of earth the necessary elements to dwell in his earthly body so long as he choose.

We found that the colour-tones of violet, modified with a soft rose red would transmute intense electrical energy if applied to the chemicals of the physical body; that these tones could be injected into the body as one might give a hypodermic injection and could ease a condition of over-stimulation at once.

Colour-tones of dove grey, combined with a misty blue, eased the nerve system and could be used as a transmitter of forces without being destructive to the nerve ends.

Yellow is a colour of freeing or releasing vital forces, permitting them to move throughout the body corporeal, transmuting as they were absorbed. This colour-tone permeated the body as sunlight.

Green in its most restful shades is a modifier of force, and can be absorbed through the pores of the skin, causing density and irritation to disappear and in their place a fine element which re-tones the cells of the body.

Silver in itself is a quickening, swift flowing stream of elixir, which elevates the whole being, transforming the blood stream as it passes through the body physical.

All the foregoing colour-tones must be used to a specific degree; man must come to know that degree in order to use it.

17 December 1955

We wish to point out that the results from the discovery of the use of the radiations as applied to the physical form did not come all at once, but were a slow, perceptive condition of response which finally brought us to the point of recognizing our Auric Being and becoming aware of it as *the Essential Entity*. Others describe this Light form as the Soul Being, the Colour form, the etheric body, but to us it is the Auric Being which carries with it the radiations which help to keep the physical body alive and well. If the radiations from the Auric Being are undeveloped, are poisoned by the thought forms projected through the mental channels, the physical, emotional vehicles will react accordingly. When the Auric Being is alight with the positive radiations, then the whole vehicle of manifestation responds in positive, active strength. This is often the case whether or not the thoughts are turned into purely religious channels. A man may feel healthy, happy and full of the powers of radiant manifestation without accepting either the moral code or the regulations laid down for him by sectarian teachings. However, he must obey the laws of his own being, and if he fails to conform to them his breaking of the laws laid down by man will be inevitable. The Auric Being is a transmitter of the light. It is a fine, delicate structure which might be likened to the web spun by a spider. Invisible lines of radiation go out from the solar body to the physical vehicle and connect through various centres to it. They are conditioned by the thought forms given but also by the receptivity of mind to the inner planes of reality. A man may not know them for what they are, may not accept them as the Triune Principle—Father, Son and Holy Spirit; may be unaware that he is a bearer of the Light in colourtone radiations, and as such creates his world of form; but in order to be such a bearer of the Light he must have an active and positive degree of receptiveness to the harmonizing qualities of being, and must share them generously with all about him. The impact of such a man upon the lives of others is frequently stronger than that of the deeply religious man. The reason is that he rarely tries to reform or condition others to his way of life because he does not channel his thought powers through a specific form, but lets them open, is friendly and outgiving.

30 December 1955

Man is prone to consider himself as predominantly a physical being. His next step is to consider himself in relation to mind and to begin to acquire mental powers. Through this step in consciousness he has begun to analyse and study the reactions of the mind upon the physical being. He has given his thought processes over to tracing the cause of disease and unrest from the psyche to the physical. We do not question this method of progress, we say it is unnecessary, at times unhealthful, but reasonable in view of man's failure to grasp the whole picture of the self in manifest form.

I am a Being of Light is a statement of fact, all is energy and energy is light. True the physical being is cast aside and finally reduced to dust and ashes, returns to earth and becomes a part of it; but Jesus taught that so to cast aside the body of manifestation is not essential, that it too may be redeemed by the very light particles of which it is composed.

Through our long periods of contemplation and study we came to see that the Light body was the reality of which the physical-mental-emotional body was merely a projection. But we also knew that the Auric Being must be developed to where it became the essential dynamo through which the physical took form, just as a vehicle of transport is empowered by a motor or dynamo or the transference of energy. We then began to classify the various aspects of the Colour-tone radiations through the Auric Being. We then knew with certainty that they composed the man, but that he had to acquire them through the use of the mind substance available to him.

Our next step was to analyse mind substance. Was it different from that which was the essential substance of being, that from which all form became manifest? We began to use our own vital energies, insofar as they could manifest through our present state of awareness. We found that the more engrossed we became in the study of the powers inherent within man the greater our capacity to visualize them. In so doing we put them to work for us; and as we did so they became dynamic and brought about results which proved to us that they were ever present faculties of being, ready to be used. We discovered the substance of being to be malleable, capable of being moulded into any form we chose.

7 January 1956

We should like to analyze further what is meant by the Auric Being, the Auric vehicle, or the man of Light:

Mind substance is generally conceived to be the mental powers of man, and it is believed by the majority that man acquires them according to his ability to grasp what has been termed generally as knowledge: namely, that which is on record and accepted by the mind of man. But knowledge is not mind substance; it is merely the ability of the ego to grasp and formulate what already is. Mind substance is the very essence of being from which all the qualities are made manifest. *It is the all-knowingness, the unlimited, the undifferentiated, the essence of all manifestation.* It is in truth that which man terms God, or the source of all good. When the mind touches upon this great cosmic awareness, it absorbs whatever it can attain to, can assimilate of light. Man has developed it throughout recorded time according to his capacity to receive, absorb and assimilate. It has colour-tone of great brilliance when fully developed. It is everlasting being, having all the potentials of the Perfect Man or Spiritual Being. It is related to the physical man as his potential manifestation. If he recognizes and acknowledges it, it becomes strong and resilient, capable of manifesting powers far beyond the ordinary. If man has not progressed to the point of recognition, it remains in abeyance until he develops the capacity for recognition; but it is always connected with the Silver Cord, or substratum of reality, which holds him within his physical body. When it is detached from the physical it acts according to its power to relate itself to another form of existence. If highly developed it moves upward into higher spheres and relates itself to the cosmic consciousness of the *all-knowing mind.* From this it gathers substance which may again return it to an earth form to give greater expression to that form or to learn lessons not previously learned.

The Auric Being, therefore, is the essence of the physical manifestation. If recognized or accepted by the manifesting body it gives off a degree of radiation (which is the equivalent of electrical energy), and which is described by those who can read or photograph the many-coloured aura.

This transformation is not the result of mental manipulation of the thought powers, but rather the result of surrender of such powers so that the body of Light may do its work without resistance. Therefore the Master taught that the man who seeks believing is the man most likely to receive the transcendent powers and become a channel for their use.

13 January 1956

We have attempted to clarify the meaning of the Auric Being, for it is so frequently misunderstood and so often referred to as the Soul or Spirit within man. Such is not the case. Man's identity as a Christed Being is formed through the auric manifestation. It is the linkage through the auric, or transmitter of the radiations, which causes him to become a spiritual being, a man of God, or the "Only Begotten". We wish to make this statement very clear.

The man Jesus, as he has told us in His own words, is not the only begotten. It is the Son of God, or the manifestation of the perfect man, which is the only begotten. It is and always will be the Spirit of God in action through the earthly vehicle, but there is a way by which it comes to know Source and to abide in it. That way is through the physical mortal being, by means of its Auric powers, or the degree of radiation of the Light energies maintained by it.

We realize that this statement will be questioned, refuted and argued over by the various schools of religious teaching, but nevertheless we bear witness to that which we have learned from the Master Himself. His statements are that He came to possess His Auric powers through many lifetimes of contacting the life-giving substance and through an Adeptship of long standing. That is, He suffered in order to bring to man the understanding of his place in relation to the God of Light, not in one manifestation alone but in many. The one of which we have a record and in which He made the total transition, demonstrating as He did so the powers of the Son of God to summon the physical or mortal body to livingness after it had been pronounced dead, was the culmination of previous lives of study, meditation and worship of the Great Over-All Radiance.

20 January 1956

The auric being manifests that which an individual has developed in the rate of his vibrations throughout his life experiences. A babe in arms may have a more highly developed auric radiation than a grown man. The fully developed aura is a thing of beauty beyond our powers of expression. Few can stand in the Presence of the Holy Ones who have developed such radiations, and few can sustain the proximity of such radiations. As man learns to absorb and assimilate the qualities of being, as they are represented through colour-tone into his auric vehicle, he becomes enlightened. His whole being is eventually irradiated and he goes to work as a server of the Light. It cannot be otherwise, for were he not to use the powers thus granted him, he would be destroyed by them.

27 January 1956

It is essential that the auric radiation be understood and that the nature of the soul or Solar Being be given its due recognition. The auric being, developed to a high degree of radiation, reflects through the so-called physical body a rate of vibration which is disturbing to the cell life and often causes one or other of the various diseases known to man. This response generally precedes the union of the physical-mental-emotional body with the spiritual or Solar manifestation. The man seems prone to illness, is tired, tense, nervous, overwrought by the demands of the Higher Self to make way for its entry in fullness through the mortal manifestation. It is then that the demands of the auric radiation become so great that the man or woman has no other recourse than to find the reason for this depletion and painful physical reaction. Such a one must use the forces evoked by continued search into Cosmic realms to build a new body, one which will carry him (or her) anywhere, into any fields of exploration, without affecting his physical, mortal being.

We found that the related colour-tones in the auric reflection were the means of maintaining such balance and that as we became overwrought and highly tense in our experiments, we could ease them by veiling our physical manifestation in a cloud of soft grey-blue; that we could seek the peace of nature by invoking the soft shades of green so manifest in its many forms; that we could make our stand in strength by invoking the fundamental blue and resting upon it as a baby might rest on a down pillow. We found that the pearly pink shades were sweet, clean and restful; that yellow in its spring flower colourings would make us joyful and tremendously free.

3 February 1956

We of course had not the problems of daily contact with the masses. We were alone in our underground cave for many days at a time. When we did see the light of day it was for the most part in conditions of bitter cold, barren wastes, hard labour and brutal supervision, so that our light could radiate only dimly and with little effect on those around us. However, it did preserve our body forms and finally became powerful enough to prevent us from having to follow the same hard schedule as these others. We were left more and more alone, considered queer and unearthly, and finally left to die of starvation. This we did not do, for by this time we had found that our sustenance came easily from the Solar substance and that we could partake of it in many ways not known to man. We were refined to the fineness of a sharpened blade. Our physical forms became barely perceptible, but our colour tone radiations were so potent that we could use them to make the many experiments which were a part of our daily practice.

The thought of food was revolting to us after we found we could assimilate from the life-giving substances all that was needful for our nourishment. But we also found that all forms of life used the same process of assimilation of the etheric substance. If they were stunted or deformed, it was because the harmonizing quality of the Solar substance radiation had not been absorbed.

10 February 1956

We found that the colour orange had a remarkable inner quality, which is both uplifting and absorbing. It revealed within its radiations a potency which enabled us to open the walls of the earth around us. We found that so much energy would be destructive were it not used in combination with a soothing, veiling flow of radiations. Orange in the cosmic acceptance of the tone may not be used in Earth man's present degree of consciousness without qualifying it by means of other radiations.

17 February 1956

As we entered deep within the bowels of the earth relics of ancient civilizations were found and, permeated by light, became alive for us. Buildings were wrought of indestructible material. They were revealed to us in jewelled colourings and stood forth against a background of colour-tone which indicated that they had been constructed by the same means by which we were able to observe them, by a process unknown to man of this period. But great rulers of such civilizations were Solar Beings who could dwell in any sphere of existence; and once the earth had been a magnificent dwelling place for such as they. The fall of man became a living thing before our eyes and we were able to envisage his past greatness and the descent of consciousness into material form, and hence into burial within that form until the time of resurrection. We could also see that these ancient lives were still potent and had a quality of livingness which must be restored to the earth which they cherished.

From these discoveries we were able to envision the "New Heaven and the new Earth". We knew without a shadow of a doubt that the unveiling of the so-called past is a fundamental part of the future of man; that all things are One, ever existent in the records as they continually unroll.

3 March 1956

We began to use the powers which were inherent within our light radiations to enter the heart of the earth, there to find a remnant of a higher civilization than the present man of earth has known. We saw that which had been built by an architect of Cosmic Realms. We understood that man had descended from a point in consciousness much higher than he could now apprehend and that from these remnants we were to learn how to build again. We knew that humanity can only build what can be conceived in consciousness; that the radiations which made it possible for us to enter the heart of the earth and discover its former glories, would help us to bring again an awareness of what has been lost like some long forgotten memory. The same creative force would enable mankind to bring about a new incarnation upon the earth of men of power and men of light, wielders of eternal substance and creators of the dream-vision in manifest form.

9 March 1956

It is an arduous path we have to tread, razor-edged, filled with difficulties because the mind is a constant betrayer of the real and most human beings come so slowly to full acceptance that they are in reality Sons of God.

It seemed to us that our incarceration underground, away from our fellow men and removed from any of the comforts of civilized living, was the ultimate in evil—"Man's inhumanity to man". Yet out of it came an expansion of consciousness which permitted us to discover that the powers inherent within man were indeed God-like. The teachings of the Master Jesus are simple. They state plainly that man is a Son of God, filled with like powers, and capable of doing anything that he believes is possible. *But he must believe.* He must take the steps to eliminate weakness, fear, doubt and the belief that he must follow the pattern set by others. His must be as individual as are his finger prints, for God made no two alike. Yet in our oneness with God we are so united that there seems to be only One—*the all-knowing Presence of Good.*

We came to see, as we found our way within the depths of the earth, that *life is ever present.* Within each clod of earth there was the substance of being, radiating life to its kind and capable of radiating it in greater degree as we brought our radiations to bear upon it. We came to see how all man's needs might be met. As he becomes one with the earth, the earth responds and gives according to what he has planted. So does the mind, or its substance, give forth that which is implanted as the *thought seed,* and manifests according to its kind.

We came to know the response of the earth, its desire to yield to man its riches, and there are riches beyond our powers to describe still held within its bosom and ready to spring forth at the touch of the understanding mind and the uniting of the qualities within the radiations of the Light. This is the next step that man must make in his progress.

16 March 1956

As we came upon the cities of ancient times, those in which man dwelt when he knew himself to be a God-like being, we found that there were many clues to the identities of those who dwell on earth today. We found evidence that we had at one time been a part of this civilization, for we could recall portions of what we found and knew ourselves to be the same beings who had helped to build them. We had endured through endless ages as beings of Light and were being restored to that which we once manifested. We also knew that incarnation in any age must be worked out according to the desire of the being to expand and endure, but always without thc help or hindrance of lessons learned in a former lifetime. We discovered that remnants of former lives must of necessity float somewhere in the consciousness, but until all lessons are learned, the whole continuity of the consciousness could not be revealed.

22 March 1956

In our experiments we found that the Solar Substance as revealed to us in its ephemeral mode was in reality a part of the resonance with which our world is filled. We also came to see that man and his earth are one and the same, the only difference being in the rate of vibration; that all was light and moving as substance became form according to the idea or image given to it. The earth was being reformed, as it were, by the manipulation of man's thought powers; but so long as he regarded it as dense matter, it could bear for him only such things as he imagined to be true. We believe that another Star is alight in the firmament, the Earth of the Christ, and as man comes to see its glory he will behold the whole Universe alight and at his disposal.

31 March 1956

As we eased into the harmonies of the higher levels of expression, we came into a colour field which helped us mightily in conquering all apparent obstacles. Release can be found in the soft spring yellow of the daffodils: behold the azure sky above, the green of spring grass beneath your feet. Feel yourself floating out gently in the soft, silvery-blue currents which mean that you are enveloped in the Light of Spirit and enjoy the time spent in whatsoever you are doing. As you come to give colour-tone a place in the pattern of your days, you will find it becomes a constant, harmonizing relationship with earth life and that of the Cosmic Field in which your work must be done.

We entered the earth domain and began to feel at home in it. Instead of being miners, we became prospectors in the heavenly lodes. We found jewels of great worth and came to understand how they came into manifestation. We discovered that we had means of communication with groups all over the earth plane, whether hidden in the earth or walking its surfaces; whether in the etheric levels which surround it, or high above it in the Cosmos. Thus we found that time and space were but relative. We came to learn how to use substance according to our desire to create form. We came to know that all is the one universe of Light, and in it we can dwell wheresoever we can build our Temple of Light.

6 April 1956

Time or place is not the conditioning influence, but the faculty of the being to lend itself to the outpouring of good. As we harmonize with the light currents above us, the lower ethers respond and harmony comes about. There is nothing that can destroy man but himself. Whatever quality of being he represents draws unto itself that quality. His consciousness must be open to new realms of being before they become real to him.

13 April 1956

Man's thought powers are his own, but whether he knows it or not he reflects that which is within the whole stream of consciousness and is affected by it. Where the consciousness is closed to the higher radiations the individual mind becomes warped and limited in its power to receive. But each degree of expansion in the consciousness of those who bear the Light elevates the whole stream of consciousness.

20 April 1956

We have spoken many times of our limiting conditions where it was not possible to escape from the confining walls imprisoning us by physical means. Our escape was shown as an interior existence. Finally we entered the very earth itself. We became aware that we need not be bound by mortal limitations, there was a vaster, more wonderful experience awaiting us. We found that we need not cast off the mortal body in order to reach realms of beauty and breadth of vision but that we were able to dwell in those qualities of being while incarcerated in a cave beneath the ground. It was thus that we began to realize that we were truly immortal. We could go from one field of conscious expression to another, finding ever greater scope. It is well for all who seek to serve to dwell in thought upon the potentials within the Creative mind. From the vantage point of a distant horizon another opens, still greater, still more wonderful. We need only seek the one immediately before us to find a greater one out-stretching, promising fulfilment in the joy of exploration.

Our findings within the heart of the Earth taught us that man knows but little of his earth plane. There are still untouched vast avenues of wealth, great volumes of wisdom, healing powers and splendours of living as yet inconceivable. Our thought for today is:

Find the self within the self. It is all powerful, all purposeful, all rewarding. Be not the victim of limitation, but its master.

27 April 1956

What we have to give is healing and vitalizing to the emotional, physical body. Little is known of the effects of the radiation on the corporeal body, yet many suffer from lack of the substance of life because they do not realize that it may be breathed in just as is the oxygen in the air. In these days all men are troubled, except those who have come to know what we have just stated. Men feel the end of a world as they have known it, and don't know what lies before them. It is difficult for the man of earth to relate himself to the whole; he sees only his individual struggle. We could not mingle with our fellow men. We caught their thought waves as they came to us by the same telepathic means by which you record. These thought waves were intensely disturbing until we came to know them for what they were and refused to identify ourselves with them. We came to know the vibrational relationships of a world of war and competition. We also came to know the vibrational response to a world of ease and harmony, one of colour-tone; one of light-filled love of all that is, which is the reality of what we term the "upper ethers".

The "upper ethers" is a realm of being far more real than that experienced by earth man, because within it lie the truth of being, the principles applicable to all of livingness, the Soul of the Universe. It is not only a way of life, *it is life itself* as it is the truth. Call it perfection, if you will, but imperfection exists only in the consciousness of man. Perfection cannot be until he has become one with the underlying idea. Many have said that it is not possible for man to realize perfection. This seems to be true in relation to his earth experience, but were he to dwell upon the idea until he felt a deep response in consciousness, he would be lifted into the higher ethers which are a part of the Divine Idea of Perfection. God the Supreme Life of all lives, knows only perfection. He sees not the failure of man to find it, but sees always the human archetype, the Son of God, and knows its livingness. From that perfect Idea stems the Christ, God within man, his own approach to the higher levels and his own redemption from the limitations, sins and destructive elements within the corporeal man.

5 May 1956

We are in no way connected with any school of thought. We believe that we are a part of the Hierarchy of Light by reason of service only. All who serve the Light faithfully and in pure desire to help their fellow men become in effect working members of that Hierarchy. Each carries out his task obediently, and as consciousness expands extends his range of activity. The Teachers of the Hierarchy transmit through many different channels whatever they wish to be made known. They do not select, nor are they represented by, any one particular or special school of thought. There are countless ways in which this is done and many channels that give no recognition whatsoever to the Hierarchical plan. These beings channel light through their belief in the Brotherhood of Man and the Fatherhood of God. God may be called by many names. His Presence may be invoked through varying beliefs, but the Light is given to whoever serves in selfless love.

We have told you that our lessons in experiment were drastic and deeply painful, all but washing away our desire to live. Only the presence of Love itself saved us from surrender to death. We had no hopes of wordly recognition, little hope that we would ever again be permitted to walk the ways of earth known or recognized by our fellow man. We were buried alive within the earth and hard labour without gain seemed to be our lot. Out of it came the belief and the faith that love and love alone could redeem the earth and make of it a place where man could dwell in peace. What we have achieved is very little in comparison with all that must yet be done before man comes to see himself as a Solar manifestation, or a Soul.

12 May 1956

Working within the earth brought forth a whole new experience. We found that life within the earth existed as strongly and positively as it does above ground. We found miracles of value to men of earth, which have not as yet been touched. We found the replicas of ancient civilizations; also jewels of rare worth and minerals as yet undreamed of by man. We found that the very substance of the depths of the earth has a rare and inexhaustible quality of life able to restore the being of man after so-called death. We found that the mineral sources within the substance of earth were such that instant growth took place under our very eyes. We found rivers of living water which when touched by our lips renewed the life current within us and through which we could transmit our forces into your world of form. We found that we were transmuted in fleshly form into beings of light without affecting the physical manifestation as it appears in outer expression. That is, that we were men as we have always been, but by touching the forces within the earth, through our desire to serve and through our love for them, we became light bodies carrying with us our mental powers and able to appraise all that was revealed to us without losing our ability to restore ourselves to physical form.

We came to feel an inner kinship with the earth as it became known to us as an urgent expression of life forces, and that man could be renewed by his contact with the earth, even though he delve into it only to make a garden grow. If he dug for minerals, going into the bowels of the earth to do so, he established a kinship with the earth which made him want to return to it. We are aware that few men know why they become miners, or how great the desire is for contact with the forces of earth, as such. But we do know that whoever enters it with a deep desire to serve humanity and in the love which must accompany such desire, he will find the qualities of life for which he has been searching. As the men of earth are now finding the wonders at the bottom of the seas, so did the men of ancient times find the wonders within the earth itself, and so can men come to know the wonders of their God and the eternal life within every particle of His substance.

16 June 1956

The whole test of the earth man is one of learning to harmonize himself with the rate of vibration of levels of consciousness bearing greater frequencies and therefore greater power to harm unless the being is in accord with the true or the good. This means that man may not be stepped up until he has learned to live in peace with his neighbour, with all forms of manifest life, and with himself most of all. Peace comes from within. Man does not pass from the physical body into a higher sphere unless he has earned that level. He does have time to review the life he has just finished and to profit by his mistakes if he has a longing in his soul to do so. Whatever he has built for the self must be worked out here or elsewhere. It is better when these things are worked out while he is in the body, for then he will have prepared himself for the harmonies which are rightfully his.

10 August 1956

The earth is now being conducted under Light Ray 3. There are rays of varying degrees of force. Under present conditions LR3 is the one which will prove most beneficial to mankind. Each Light Bearer is used as a spearhead for the incoming forces. Each has a mission peculiar to his own channelling powers, and all together the reflection of the radiations brings about etheric, atmospheric, as well as personal changes in the lives of men. The earth experience is a vast one involving not only human life, but animal, vegetable and mineral kingdoms as well. Man may have established home or community upon the earth surface as at present, but he may also have his secret abiding place within its activated depths, where he may draw sustenance from the wealth of raw material available for his use. As man continues to work with radiation in its ever increasing manifestation he will come to know that "as man thinks so is he"; that his thought forces may take him into the ethers whence he may draw radiations which will be very helpful in the new phase of his consciousness.

17 August 1956

As you respond to our recording and we respond to your vibrational capacity to do so, an acceleration in the light degree takes place which, if properly prepared for, harmonizes all the vehicles. One does not balance the etheric, physical emotional and mental bodies without practising the art of so doing. It has to be learned, just as one learns to play a musical instrument by long and arduous practice.

At this time in the history of the earth it is well to consider that the demand is great, but the reward is greater. The earth itself is in process of change. Nature and animal life are reflecting the etheric radiation. Many animals are beginning to have a common field of exchange. As these animals are developed, so will the vegetable and mineral life respond and become very positive in their response to the demands made upon them.

You are recording the steps in transition from one form of consciousness to another. We in turn are experimenting and investigating the potentials within such change. We know by our own tests that the mineral, animal and vegetable kingdoms are readily receptive to the thought forces. A flower will open quickly to the thought of love, just as does an animal. A vegetable will grow quickly and into perfect form when attended by loving hands, and the reverse is also true. The earth warmed by the Sun responds and quickens, not only because of the warmth, but by reason of the radiations it contains. When parched and dry it responds instantly to water, which is the reflection of the life substance.

In order to grasp each quality of being in its essential meaning, one must come to know and understand the spiritual counterpart. Mankind need not know poverty, fear, distress, physical or mental, if man will but learn the simple truths of being as he learns the alphabet. He need not know death if he would learn the meaning of life.

7 September 1956

As the Light Bearer becomes responsive to the Light he is raised to a position in the Cosmos where he is able to help to stabilize the Forces of Light. Each of us must consider that we are outposts in the Cosmic realm, used to transmit the Light waves throughout all manifest form. Whatever our place in the great scheme, to balance the rhythm is our privilege and within our power.

In working within the earth we have been called upon to accept the potentials of the Light Body and to use it as we would a magic cloak. This means that we accept it as our reality; that we call upon it to work for us; that we assume it as the Self of ourselves, and in so doing command it to our purposes. Perhaps we can make this clearer for you by reminding you of the miracles wrought by the Master Jesus as He permitted the Body of Light to take charge. Before he could do so it was necessary for him to command the lesser self, or the man of earth, to get out of the way. He accepted the crucifixion because he knew that in so doing the body of Light would be able to take charge and He could then manifest at will. He gave recognition to the truth that the Body of Light was His reality, the physical form merely a facet of His expression. Nevertheless it was necessary for Him to put this truth to the proof so that man could come to understand that he is more than mortal; that he is indeed a Son of God and capable of doing the things done by the Master, "and even greater things".

As we explore the magic of the earth workings from within, we come to realize the magic manifest in the outer. Deep within is the pulse of the earth manifestation. It comes from the inner essence of the form and brings forth the fruits of the earth on demand. But man cannot experience the greater good until he has called it forth by the powers inherent within him as a reflection of the Most High.

The tests are many and severe that the aspiring pupil has to make: first he must overcome the unreality of his material existence, while still living and subject to the daily demands and constant imperfections of the earth realm. Nevertheless, as he comes to know the perfect he comes to live in it and in so doing helps others to find the way. As man comes into knowledge of his own powers as a son of Light he will elevate the powers of all life expressions.

Mankind is not as yet free from bondage, even actual slavery, and while in your country [*the United States*] freedom is proclaimed as the essence of its constitution, yet no man is free while he is still bound to the belief that material possessions are the mark of his progress upon earth. Therefore he must repeat his earth experience over and over again. Having ourselves been in slavery, subjected to enforced labour under the greatest duress, we know that only the Solar experience can set man free. Living the soul life may not be entirely understood. It is the essence of being, it must be regarded as the highest awareness of being that man can have, must bc accepted as his reality, and his earth-plane existence as merely a testing of his understanding of that reality.

26 October 1956

We have become sufficiently enlightened to act as reflectors or screens for the needs of those capable of communicating with us, and who are sympathetically aligned with our work. Many scientists are so aligned, although they do not know the service given or the nature of the work done by us. They feel a strong, impelling urge to focus their forces upon some one particular form of experiment and intuitively call upon us to help them. This call is flashed until the necessary alignment is made. We, in turn, channel our perceptive powers towards their experiment and as we do so results follow both for them and for us. What we are in effect doing is adding our powers to theirs and as it is doubled or trebled, as the case may be, they find themselves with a solution undreamed of, or possibly an entirely new concept. Our powers are enhanced as well. We do not claim that we are the creators of the result, but we have learned that as we add our gifts to those of the creative artists, in whatever field, we enhance the speed and power of the results. Hence your many recent activities into the upper ethers which will result eventually in a meeting of the minds of earth with those of other planets.

Within the earth's surfaces are undreamed-of possibilities, potentials of such magnitude that earth man could literally levitate his physical body from one plane to another were he to become conscious of the potentials within this field of experiment. The awareness of Solar Substance and its infinite usefulness in advancing the cause of man, is one of the discoveries. Solar Substance is the potential of all manifestation, but it has many forms and the radiance within the earth causes a great wealth of material to be made available for man's use. Meditation upon the life-giving values of Solar Substance is a splendid way to open consciousness to its uses.

23 November 1956

"Thou shalt not kill" is a fixed law of human life. Lessons in experience have so far not taught man that he cannot kill lest he be killed, but those who break the commandment are not the only one who suffer. All humanity suffers by the misuse of Principle. Now at this point of consciousness upon our earth plane the crucifixion is imminent. The whole of humanity must carry the cross to Golgotha and die to its evils that it may live again to the good.

Many are now being sent to us for restoration. They are released from their imprisoned bodies but do not know where to go. They see a light and seek us out. Then come the periods of restoration, sometimes long when the body is old and wearied of its burdens, sometimes short when the soul has elevated the body consciousness into the Light. Such as these are quickly transmitted in their Light bodies to a place where their work may be continued. From there they instruct and aid their suffering comrades. Car-loads of humans come in as cattle to the hovels surrounding us. If they survive that ordeal in the physical body they have to endure even worse. But in the caves where we, and those who are aligned with us, have our being, classes of instruction are now going on. Those who can join us physically do so. Those who cannot are treated in their Solar consciousness until they are able to think for themselves. Many of these are the victims of the recent carnival of horror in Hungary. Many have given up hope and faith seems dead. It is not dead, nor are they. They need only to be revived by the Everlasting Presence of the One Magnificent Demonstrator of Light Eternal. He is with us in radiation and in presence much of the time. A gentle touch of His hand and the being is restored. Frequently they feel His radiations and come to life again to renew their faith, and to transmit their radiations to suffering humanity. Children are most easily quickened. They are so filled with love that they transmit themselves in light forms to help the older ones who are broken in mind and body. Angels of Light, wearing crowns in honour of their service, seek to help us and everywhere around the darkened scene bands of enlightened souls come to help.

7 December 1956

The heart is often cruelly torn by the vicissitudes of daily life, but where it is filled with the Christ love it cannot be harmed. There is always a way and that Way is to turn to the indwelling One and place the burden upon His shoulders. His love and strength can and will carry it for you.

Many go up and down in the scale of their awareness, balanced sometimes precariously between the two realms of being, longing for the heights, yet dwelling within the depths. This is a part of mortal experience. We cannot conquer by abandoning the life around us, but rather by bringing to it those qualities of being which restore and invigorate.

14 December 1956

Mortal responses to the Fields of Light are strange. At times the radiations are more than the being, torn between two worlds, can stand. He feels shattered, with no place in reality. Those of earth, and close to the material manifestation, have no roots, or so it seems. But those who have elected to serve in the Light and Love of Christ are more often weary wanderers on the planes of physical manifestation.

Peace be unto your physical, mental and emotional bodies. They are but channels for the Solar Radiance and as they expand to receive it, they stretch ever upward into Cosmic realities.

We are buoyed by the radiance which has been invoked around us. We also meet the Master face to face and His powers are ours insofar as we can accept them. You too have the same privilege. Make clear the way for that which is to illumine the minds and hearts to still greater giving. One resentful thought may create disease and unrest within the auric manifestation, for it is alien to the Life Eternal.

While we are in the process of achieving mastery the lessons to be learned more often than not seem unbearable, yet they are a part of our experience in the earth world and when once learned need never be repeated. Beware of accepting *karma* not yours. Each member of any given group must learn to stand alone. Unknowingly they will draw upon you for sustenance, yet there must never be a giving of the forces of the being, each must learn to engender his own energies and to manifest them for the good of others. One should not sustain another who has sufficient understanding to learn to stand alone, neither is it wise to project one's forces toward one who is not ready for them. Each will learn his or her own lessons through experience over many incarnations. We have had to learn ours through great testings and more often than not through experiences seemingly impossible to man. We have probed into the darkened depths of earth itself, and penetrated them by our radiant beams. We claim them not as personal attainments, but rather we acknowledge them once and forever as the reflection of the Christ Mind, the All Knowing Radiation.

22 December 1956

We draw from the earth, deep within its heart, the matrix of the physical manifestation. Few give recognition to the powers inherent within the material body of the earth. They are hidden there until the time comes when man can find and renew himself with them. They are revealed to all who search with the aim of fulfilling a mission of redemption and restoration.

Many before us have so searched, more will do so, for awareness is creeping into the consciousness of man and he is beginning to know that the plane of his physical existence may indeed become the plane of his heavenly realities. But first must come the cleansing, and it is for this that we work and because of this we suffer disease, disharmony, carry the cross of humanity through the black night of transition. We feel no grief, for did not our Master do the same? What He came to exemplify we came to carry on: thus are we made whole in His sight.

Long ago the Atlanteans, the Aztecs and various tribes that followed them, learned the secrets of manifesting through so-called density. To conquer the air, the earth's atmospheres, is by far easier than to learn to dwell within it.

But the Radiances can and do take the Solar Being wherever it desires to be. On them we are transported. In them we live and move and have our being. Because of them a stone may be rolled away from a tomb, a body which has undergone death be restored to life. The Master knows and teaches the mystical laws of Being when the pupil is ready to surrender the whole of self through the living of the Law.

28 December 1956

Few realize just what is now taking place on earth. Changes in every form of life are manifest. Deep within the heart of the earth itself comes the impulse to a greater growth, a fuller life expression. Within the various strata of matter, as it appears below the surface, are elements which are now becoming available for man's use, and which will change the whole of the globe as they become recognized. They have begun a transmutation of the natural forms. Vegetation is fast disappearing on some surfaces to be replaced by mineral content which will transform the living qualities of the earth. In other desert places will come a form of vegetation which will cause them to "bloom like the rose", and will bring to the surface waters of great value in the healing of disease in both man and animal. Mountains will produce minerals of such great value to the life on the planet that the struggle for material wealth will depart. Money will have no value because it will no longer be the medium of exchange.

The Earth's atmospheres are even now rapidly changing, and if war in its most destructive form can be prevented our air or atmosphere will become purified. Exchange between planets of useful information will be possible, for the very work now done in transmission of ideas from one level to another is to stimulate the use of telepathic transmission. This in itself will most rapidly enlighten the minds of men and will cause them to elevate the consciousness more easily into Cosmic levels. All of this will take place as the result of man's desire to banish the evils he has created, and to serve only the good.

11 January 1957

At present we are working most diligently with the radiation applied to the mental-physical being of those who have been deported and enslaved. The radiations are injected by a special method into such wanderers between realms and will in time evoke a response so that the soul may continue to manifest through its physical being. In some cases release from the physical takes place and the Soul becomes aware of its faculties and regenerates into active planes of consciousness. We shall attempt to explain this.

The almost unbearable struggle, the physical weakness, combined with a feeling on the part of some patients that the struggle is not worth while, causes a deterioration of both mind and body. In such cases the patient is gently treated by the silvery-blue Ray, wherein the Solar Being is enhanced, but no attempt is made to inject the radio-active radiance. Radio-active radiances are those colour-tone beams which are highly energized and a specific degree indicated for use in treatment. The silver-blue Radiance may be so activated, but in cases where the patient is largely detached from the physical, the silvery-blue may be used as a releaser rather than an activator of the mental-physical processes. We are attempting to express our findings in your language and it may not be as clear as we would wish it to be. What do you feel, for instance, when you become aware of even an infinitesimal amount of the Love Ray? Is it not warming like sunlight? Quickening, like the flow of quicksilver, soothing, uplifting, sustaining, tranquilizing, each of which quality has a colour tone reflection? The Solar powers may be used to induce whatever state of consciousness is desirable for the being, but he must make the choice. There is never any compulsion.

When the being wishes to depart from the physical shell, we send the tranquilizing, relaxing and releasing radiances within the silver-blue. They also inspire and uplift until the release is made and the soul is free to wing its way to another sphere. It may be seen leaving the body and ascending in flight. In flight it will make contact with the particles of radiation necessary to sustain it until it has found form in the sphere to which it has been directed. There may be no earth memory, or it may be quickly returned, depending entirely upon the use of and receptivity towards the Solar Radiation.

18 January 1957

There are times when even the most spiritually minded feel that the body form is without animation, a shell with little besides painful memories and discomfort. When this is the case, usually a step is being made into the Cosmic realms and the being is preparing for a greater work. It is wise at such times to drop all thought of striving, to relax and release in the Presence and let the knowledge that one is never apart from the Supreme Power infiltrate the whole being.

The use of Colour tone radiation has many functions, among them to restore the magical qualities of Being and thus release them. To learn how to use them to help others is to learn how to live as a Solar Being, aware of the perfection of the Life of Spirit, yet able to step into the depths of hell, as it were, and release those who are prepared to receive the radiations from Above. All men must receive their purification through a purgatorial cleansing. There is no escape from that which has been built by the body of mankind through their thought projections. One may not have committed an especial sin, but if his brother has done so and he seeks to help his brother, he may in turn pay his own *karmic* debt in absolution for that sin. In other words, man pays for all the evils of mankind in one way or another. This is the teaching of the Master Jesus. He showed us by example how it might be done. What He also taught us was that by the use of the Heavenly Fire, the radiations of the Light, healing could take place instantly and man no longer have to suffer the fires of purification. But only when all men are lifted up.

Our intent is to point the way for the practice of the use of the radiations. We come slowly to learn that there *is a way,* a perfect path which will prevent the reaction of pain from the ills of the body of mankind. We take this path by believing in it and by practising the use of the Radiations. We come to know what Colour Tone means, what the Essence of Being is, that we are natural inheritors of the healing forces, and as we come to mingle our vibrations with them we come to know that all life is a healing force. We have but to become one with it and the ills of mind and body fall away into nothingness. *We are the Perfect Body in the Christ of God.*

Many outward manifestations of the Christ and His Kingdom upon the Earth are now being revealed, not only through Messengers of Light, but through those who seem to be earth children and with but little previous preparation for the Light. Sometimes through bodies wracked with pain and suffering the Light descends and the being is made whole. Sometimes in the midst of evil and despair, the being lifts his head and beholds the Christ. Many times in suffering caused by great sacrifice, the being sees within his own vehicle of manifestation the Living Christ and gives thanks that it is so.

25 January 1957

Man is becoming attuned to his higher vibrations and is bringing forth the fruit of his attempts to do so in the form of help to those who have not as yet made such attempts. "If I be lifted up I shall draw all men unto me." That statement is now being demonstrated as a truth for all men, not just one. Each by his vibrational response to the radiation uplifts the consciousness. His proximity to the one who receives the vibration matters little. This may be so, or it may be purely a matter of sending, or projecting, the Radiations. There is but one Power, and that Power is constantly winging its way through space. Wherever it is absorbed and activated in a stream of consciousness it elevates, transfigures and transmutes.

Accepting the premise that the Colour Tone radiations are the basic qualities of being, and that as such they are a perfect reflection of such qualities, they can be used and blended into forms of healing power. What more is there to healing the ills of man than the use of the radiations of Pure Being?

1 February 1957

Those who have striven to rise above the general consciousness also rise above the astral and are protected by the descending radiations. As opposed to the astral we have the etheric consciousness which is a blend of man's higher ideals and aspirations according to his ability to interpret the perfect or absolute truth of being. The etheric ascent is a constant expansion and tends to keep the faculties of the being in balance between emotional and mental levels. The more emotional the being, the more receptive he becomes to the astral reflection. Thus often buried deep within his consciousness are forms of illness, impurity, neglect of self, and other deeply disturbing psychoses which need to be eradicated before the individual in question can partake of the etheric thought forms.

When we speak of emotional, we speak of a response to vibrational waves. Man may be extremely intellectual and yet be deeply subject to waves of thought from astral levels. He may be mentally geared to forceful thinking, yet if he is open and responsive psychically to disturbing waves of thought, he is not capable of reaching into the sphere of clear, intelligent reasoning, which has its base in fundamental principles of being. It is for this reason that a way of erasing or eradicating the responsiveness to destructive thought forces is sought. Many of your trained hypnotists are aware of this and use their powers constructively to eradicate thought forms of illness, belief in subconscious evils, reflection of astral plane thought forces, which are deeply destructive to the sensitive psychic body of man.

There is much yet to be learned and much to be overcome in the race thought before a correction can be made in the psychic body of man. We are rapidly approaching that point by the injection of radiation throughout the earth's ethers. The radiation corrects and cures automatically, but only if it is received by a healthy consciousness, one that is cleared of past *karmic* influences, purified of erroneous thought habits, and ready to surrender the whole of the self to the higher vibrations. But man cannot attain that point of surrender wholly through his own self-conscious thinking. He must be prepared for it by a cleansing and purifying of his emotional-psychic vehicles. He will then be ready to raise his separate consciousness, and consciousness of separation, and to blend it with the Supernal Consciousness.

24 May 1957

Our desire is to bring to you further understanding of our work which is being done by the Overlighting Ones as they perceive the great need. Again the testing point has been reached and the Earth itself is threatened with disaster. This is apparent in many ways and cannot be measured in terms of reports of disaster to separate portions of the Planet, or to individuals or groups of people. These are only a reflection of the long mis-directed thought forces of man.

We should like, however, to speak upon a subject which has been causing difference of opinion. The militarist and the run-of-the-mill scientists still claim that no harm has been done by atomic tests; that the fall-out is not sufficient to injure mankind, and so they continue under blind misapprehension of the character of the forces now inplayed by such tests. Man and his earth are in mortal danger from such tests, the shock from which may cause portions of the planet to disappear and may also react upon the emotional-mental fibre of man, demoralizing the inner core of his response to earth plane living. This is evident in the increase in mental breakdown through shock to the systems of those who are emotionally sensitive and also in the shock to the responsive nature of mankind as a whole. Because the actual fibre of man's being is not given recognition, either by the religions or the scientist, there is little recognition given to the shock to which it is being submitted. But until man is able to build for himself his Body of Light, strong and invincible, he is a creature between planes, so it seems, and is profoundly affected by the etheric condition of his Earth World. It is there that the threat lies, not in what he believes or refuses to believe, but in the actual conditions of his etheric environment which are in turn the result of erroneous thought forms.

Those who overlight know the cure. They know that if a man would accept the concept of a world overlighted by a Supreme Being capable of conceiving only good, would believe that from this Supernal One come the radiations to restore and rebuild, would take to their hearts the love which will cause them to reach out to the very heart of Being, then the earth might be saved from the evil forces now pounding at the fibre of man's being.

We cannot over-emphasize the necessity for acceptance of the God-Consciousness, the Spiritual Substance from which man is formed. Here and now is the time. Here and now the privilege of so serving that a great wave of enlightenment inform the minds of men, uplift their consciousness, opening the petals of the heart to resound to Love and the mind to Light.

Four Letters from *Light*

Four Letters from *Light*

From: Kathleen Raine

Readers of *Light* cannot fail to be impressed by the remarkable scripts, purporting to come from Russian prisoners, of which a first instalment appeared in the Winter issue, and a further section in the present issue. The editorial foreword to the first section expressed the view of the majority of the *Light* editorial committee, whose discussion took place when I was out of the country. The editor has kindly allowed me this opportunity of registering my own doubts, not about the extraordinary interest of the script, but about its interpretation. On the analogy of many communications, from Swedenborg to the present, in which communicators were unaware of the fact that they had "died", is not one possible alternative interpretation of these scripts that they record discarnate experiences of a group unaware of the fact that their life is no longer corporeal? In a Marxist society, where it is taught that the material world is all, is there not a strong possibility that those who find themselves continuing to exist would naturally conclude that they could not have died?

This is of course only a possibility—there is no way of proving the matter one way or the other. But above all we must refrain from jumping to hasty conclusions. Credulity and incredulity are the Scylla and Charybdis barring any true voyage of discovery in these mysterious worlds.

From: Rosamond Lehmann

My friend and colleague Kathleen Raine suggests "one possible alternative interpretation" of *A World Within a*

World. I respect her views but cannot share them. Indeed, had I done so, I would never have offered these enigmatic scripts for publication.

Far from "jumping to hasty conclusions" I have had them in my possession, read, re-read and pondered on them for over eleven years. They came into the hands of Sir George Trevelyan in somewhat mysterious circumstances during one of his week-end seminars at Attingham Park (I think in 1967). An anonymous someone, still unidentified by him, had placed a fairly battered-looking quarto batch of typescript on his desk, saying merely that it must be given to him. At the close of the seminar, when it was his wont to mention various new writtings relevant to our studies, he brought this one to our attention. At that time I was Chairman of the PEN Writers in Prison Committee, and when he spoke of tortured Russian prisoners of conscience, I quickly asked if I might take it. He handed it to me forthwith.

Later in the day, when I came to read it, its impact overwhelmed me: "awestruck" is not too strong a word. I felt that I had been entrusted with a treasure of incalculable value. But what to do with it? How, when, where to make it public? I showed it to Cynthia Sandys, whose reaction corroborated mine; later to Paul Beard; and in the last year of his life to W. Tudor Pole. He vouched for the prisoners' authenticity, giving me to understand, though with his customary caution, that tidings of this incarcerated group had already reached him, and adding that all of them had now left their imprisoned bodies. Otherwise, rightly or wrongly, I spoke of them to no one until some months ago, when, sensing that the time was ripe at last, I presented them at an Editorial Board meeting. It was agreed to publish them in three issues of *Light*.

I knew of course that Kathleen Raine agreed with me about the value of the scripts; at the time, her strong reservations regarding their interpretation were unrealized by me. However, I am well aware of the pitfalls in the field of interpretation; but intuitive, subjective elements are bound to enter in: attunement to the "wavelength"; above all, imagination: all these *must* play a part in assessing such a document as this.

Why should members of a Marxist society, "taught that the material world is all", therefore presumably not dissidents, *be* entombed, persecuted? Who taught them to love God? To pray? To recognize and reverence Him whom they call the Master Jesus? To accept a discipline and training in spiritual alchemy, or if you like, the transmutation of ray-energies, of almost unbelievable precision and intensity? Did they undergo a post-mortem Pauline conversion in the twinkling of an eye? And if they were discarnate, why record the healing of bodily sores and the overcoming of their bodily necessity for food?

I would never claim to be able always to steer correctly between credulity and incredulity; but, as Dr. Johnson somewhere remarks: "Human experience, which is constantly contradicting theory, is the great test of truth"; and I venture to say, in all humility, that the Blue Light is known to me. I have experienced it. At a time of unutterable affliction, I was surrounded and sustained by an essence, almost a substance, of unearthly blue, throughout the worst days. A grace? A mystery? Impossible? But so it was, part of what I live by, as I have written elsewhere.*

Perhaps it was this experience that inclined me to an initial response to the present unique group testimony, although in the absence of further factual information the strangeness, the mystery, remain. Also, doubtless an area of controversy, since every new, dynamically creative act or concept, in any field of knowledge, generates disturbance or resistance. But to my own inner ear (not only to mine, of course) this concerted document is stamped with the very opposite of psychic fantasy. It is concrete, solid—heavy going, in fact: but it is living, *real*; scientific in its accumulation and presentation of tested and re-tested

* *The Swan in the Evening. Wm. Collins, London, 1967. Soon to appear in paperback (Virago).*

esoteric findings. In my view, it demands very serious attention.

(1) See also Jung's experience of the Blue Light in the tomb of Galla Placidia. (*Memories, Dreams, Reflections*, p. 314).

From: Paul Beard

It is impossible because of difficulties of time and space to authenticate *A World within a World* in documentary terms. It will continue to raise problems as to how it really came about.

There are four possible sources: (1) by telepathy from living Russian prisoners; (2) by such persons when discarnate; (3) imagined entirely by the sensitive; (4) drawn from the sensitive's deeper mind whilst in tune to some degree with archetypal patterns of spiritual transformation, and given innocently as a narrative, though really symbolic.

The scripts do not seem to me likely to arise from a discarnate mind confused as to its whereabouts. They equate better with many descriptions of out-of-body experiences by living persons who have found themselves passing through the walls of their room, and out beyond. Consciousness then appears to become dissociated and to function at etheric level. Nor are the scripts characteristic of experiences soon after death. If we accept the evidence we have of these, spiritual receptivity at such a level is unlikely to arise simultaneously with what would then be illusions of confining prison walls and starvation diet; the one state does not go readily with the other. In a nation with a religious history like that of Russia, it is not hard to accept that some prisoners, whatever the reason for their having fallen foul of the regime, could be ready to undergo a spiritual experience; and indeed the privations and near-starvation of prison have a likeness to religious austerities undergone in the hope of receiving ecstasies.

All transmissions necessarily take on subjective elements from the sensitive's mind. However conscientious and well-intentioned, the medium is deprived of any opportunity to check the material objectively.

What the scripts portray is a change and raising of consciousness. As such they might be reflecting what each of us in our own way will ultimately undergo on earth or beyond. If the sensitive has tuned into such a level, and then with another part of her mind clothed it as happening to imaginary Russian prisoners, this would be disturbing to those who think the psychic field is a simple one. However, it would not deprive the scripts of the genuine spiritual content they have brought to a number of readers. It *would* involve being careful not to make claims with undue confidence.

Each reader bears the responsibility of judging this difficult material for himself, allowing others to judge in turn in the same way.

From: Brenda Marshall

After the first instalment of *A World Within a World* appeared in *Light*, it was brought to our notice that an interview with Peter Caddy had appeared in *Onearth 5* (Findhorn, Spring 1978) in which these scripts were clearly referred to (hitherto unknown to the Editorial Board). While this of course does not "authenticate" the scripts, references in the interview with Peter Caddy link up with my own direct knowledge (i.e. from some of the people concerned, now no longer in the body) of sustained and concerted work by groups of remarkable individuals in different parts of the world dedicated to contacting and transmitting higher levels of consciousness: some results of which (including the projection of light through walls; and—though this is impossible to describe—the projection of love as a force) I have direct knowledge of. For this reason, I consider the scripts to have connection with the spiritual work of individuals while in the body.

It seems to me that a sensitive of this kind, tuning in telepathically to the unknown, would receive also impressions from the global thoughtform; and even, if she had the calibre, impressions or reflections of impressions in the mind of the Hierarchy—i.e. the thought-forms which the Hierarchy are trying to bring into manifestation on earth. Others devoting their energies in a concerted attempt to earth these blueprints may well have included prisoners of conscience in Russia. To me this presents a spectrum with unmanifested Truth at one end and human limitation at the other; it would seem that some are resonating to the higher levels of this spectrum and finding affinity with this spiritual impulse. The scripts may well be a (necessarily very imperfect) part of an attempt to earth higher energies, to awaken certain thought-forms in the human mind. One thing is certain from the response they have aroused: they have an inherent energy.

Readers may be interested in *Vedic Psychism* by Jeanine Miller (*Light,* Summer 1975), which gives an insight into light and sound as creative forces.

Vedic Psychism

Vedic Psychism

JEANINE MILLER

Psychism, which derives its name from the Greek *psyche* or soul, is, strictly speaking, the science of the psychic centres and their use. Psychology which should have made the human soul its special study merely examines the workings of the mind and denies the very existence of that which stands behind the mind and uses it. So Carl Jung, the greatest psychologist of our century, made the ironic remark:

> "We can perhaps summon up courage to consider the possibility of a 'psychology with the psyche,' that is a theory of the psyche ultimately based on the postulate of an autonomous, spiritual principle." (*Structure and Dynamics of the Psyche,* p. 344.)

Such a psychology with the psyche goes back in India to prehistoric times, indeed it was known in Vedic times. From the four original sacred scriptures of ancient India, the Vedas (the Rgveda, the oldest and most revered, the Yajurveda, the Samaveda and the Atharvaveda) which are a collection of hymns taking us to a very remote age before our Christian era, it is possible to gain an idea of the Vedic sages' remarkable insight into the intricacies of the psyche.

To the Vedic bards the world was fundamentally threefold and thus also was man (the microcosm of the macrocosm, cf. St. Paul):

(1) Heaven, or the shining Father (Dyaus from div to shine, hence deva the shining one).
(2) The middle region (antariksha: antar=within, middle; iksha=viewed).
(3) Earth (prthivi from prth—to extend. Matter is extension, hence earth is the material or terrestrial world).

The field of psychic experience is thus the middle region (viewed from within) antariksha, a word which scholars, not understanding its fundamental meaning, translate as the atmosphere or firmament. This middle field of human experience includes clairvoyance (extra-sensory seeing), clairaudience (extra-sensory hearing), psychometry, telepathy, etc. Our physical senses are in fact but the outer projection of our psychic senses which may be dormant or inhibited through an over-active intellect, but are nevertheless present. The Vedic sages called the senses the godly powers of which the king, the co-ordinator, was the mind. The soul's faculty par excellence is not the mind but what we express as intuition and the Hindus as buddhi, which operates quite apart from the mind and flashes forth an entrance into that mysterious core of the soul which St. Paul named the spirit, which Meister Eckhardt called the apex of the soul, and the Indian sages the atman.

The realm of the psyche is like a crossroads; it is a gateway that may open the door to the deepest insight to which man can have access, but such an access depends solely upon himself—and the grace of the Spirit.

The science of the psyche should lead man to discover within himself that which is his origin and his goal, his birth-right and his fulfilment, namely the Spirit, his ground of being, his security, his salvation. The ultimate question ever remains: do we want *Truth*, i.e. that which lies beyond the lure of all the senses and their deceptiveness, for whether they are physical or psychic, outer or inner, all the senses are deceptive, or do we want only phenomena?

The Vedic bards were seers. They wanted the Truth, but they were prepared to go the full length of thorough investigation in the middle region.

One factor of supreme importance to the understanding of the Vedic science of the soul is thus seership. The sages claimed that they saw the Vedas. This means fundamentally that the Rgveda, e.g., is not a collection of hymns of purely imaginative purport but the poetic expression of supersensuous, visionary experiences; it sings by way of myth, of allusions and aspirations, the inner life of the psyche.

We should distinguish two main aspects of seership; that which takes place at the psychic or intermediate level, which views the multiplicity of noumena underlying phenomena and on which was based the ritual life of all prehistoric societies; and that which takes place at the mystic level, i.e. that which goes far deeper, piercing through the multiplicities of appearances to their one underlying factor or principle, giving rise to the vision of oneness, the great characteristic of all the mystics of all races and creeds and ages. The famous Rgvedic verse,

"To what is essentially one in being poets give many names" (X.114.5) is a typical example.

A note of warning as to seership in general should be sounded. The Mahatma Letters to A. P. Sinnett point out quite clearly:

> "There is one general law of vision (physical and mental or spiritual), but there is a qualifying special law proving that all vision must be determined by the quality or grade of man's spirit and soul. . . ."

In other words, what a man will see depends largely upon the quality or purity of his vehicles—his soul, his mind, his senses, psychic and physical. No two men's vision or insight can be exactly alike. Furthermore

> "There is but one general law of life, but innumerable laws qualify and determine the myriads of forms perceived and of sounds heard. . . . Unless regularly initiated and trained—concerning the spiritual insight of things . . . no self-tutored seer or clairaudient ever saw or heard quite correctly."
>
> (Mahatma Letters, London, 1924, p. 255.)

We may strongly surmise that the Vedic bards were trained. The evidence in the Rgveda itself points to a golden age of seership whose continuity does not seem to have been broken. A well-marked trend in the hymns not to break with tradition is reflected in the hints as to the handing down from generation to generation of certain secret knowledge through which the bards traced their line of descent to an actual figure, or figures, in fact, to the seven primeval sages of mythical lore. Such continuity both at the physical and spiritual level was a proof to them of the firm foundation of their science.

> So the bards request the seven primeval sages to help them to "give birth . . . to pious men.
> May we be sons of heaven, and with our shining forth, may we break through the treasure-holding mountain-rock."
>
> (IV.2.15.)

The Rgveda is so full of references to treasure mountain-caves that one is tempted to compare these with what the Lord God says in Isaiah:

> "And I will give thee the treasures of darkness and the hidden riches of secret places." (45:3.)

The essential idea contained in both these verses is that in the stillness, and the darkness, and the emptiness of the heart, the cave of the human being, the flame-spirit, the solar deity, the Christ-child is brought to birth. With our "shining forth" we break through the rock of enfolding matter, we pierce beyond the sub-conscious until the inner divine spark is brought to manifestation, "shines forth" through us.

Through the study of Vedic meditation we can discover the fundamentals of the Vedic science of the psyche; meditation meant with the Vedic bards absorption in sound and light, the sound emitted by the human voice, the light flashed by the soul through the thought process, and their eventual transcendence, whence the core of the soul was reached. Hence we have mantric meditation, visual meditation, and supreme illumination.

I. Sound, as we understand it, is only the outer expression of an inner power of whose infinite potency we have no idea. The great Masters of the past knew that every state of consciousness finds expression as a fundamental vibration, and every vibration necessarily affects states of consciousness. Particular states of consciousness can thus be brought about by initiating particular kinds of sound.

Experiments have nowadays been carried out with sound and we know how harmonious music has an integrating effect upon humans, animals and plants, and its opposite a disintegrating effect.

"Every life-form"—whether it be a grain of sand or a highly complex human being—"has its own inner vibrational life, its own inner sound," writes the violinist, Herbert Whone in his *The Hidden Face of Music*. This inner sound is the song of each particle of life. Its nature implies

> "a frequency complex, a harmonic superstructure unique to each living being. . . . In fact, if we know at what rate a particular life-form is vibrating, we have control over, and insight into, that being. When a glass is sympathetically resonated, its fundamental tone can be heard to sing out; but we have only to increase the intensity of that resonating force to over-stimulate the glass and disintegrate it."

(cf., the walls of Jericho falling at the sound of the trumpets, and Daniel's harp soothing Saul's disturbed psyche.)

Sound is a creative force, the power inherent in the Logos. But the sound our ears register is only the coarsest manifestation of that Logos. As the Rgveda has it, the divine VAC was meted out in four sections; that which man hears is only the fourth and lowest of these and each one corresonds to a particular level of manifestation.

Herbert Whone points out:

> "When a sound in the physical world is uttered, there is interpenetration at all levels . . ." (p. 22).

Because

> "The Logos sound (has) condensed and become locked in a particular form and there is a correspondence between

> the sound uttered on this physical level and the Logos intelligence level. The key back to the original non-involved state of a given form lies in its own vibrational structure." (p. 25).

We have here the secret of sound in a nut shell, a secret more than touched upon in the Secret Doctrine of the much maligned H. P. Blavatsky:

> "Esoteric science teaches that every sound in the visible world awakens its corresponding sound in the invisible realms and arouses to action some force or other on the occult side of nature." (Vol. V, p. 431.)

But the Vedic bards discovered a peculiarity about the emitting of words: to sound a word or note was to emit a light; that which sounds in the ether is visible; sound vibrates as colour, colour vibrates as sound. To shine forth a prayer or sing it forth is equivalent. In chanting our praises, our love for God, we shine forth our truth. A great 19th century Advaita Vedantist claimed that the Vedas had two meanings, one being the sense of the words, the other indicated by the metre and the intonation.

> "Learned pandits and philologists of course deny that intonation has anything to do with philosophy or ancient esoteric doctrine, but the mysterious connection between intonation and light is one of the (Vedas') most profound secrets."
>
> "Every sound," says the Secret Doctrine, "corresponds to a colour and a number, a potency spiritual, psychic or physical." (Vol. V, p. 431.)

Such prayers as the Vedic hymns, accompanied by the illuminations of wise insight, were considered as anointing the gods to whom they were addressed and as quickening both in gods and men a response to loftier thought which in turn brought the human worshipper in harmony with truth, truth being the originating source and the ground of being.

The power of sound in audible prayer is called mantra. The "sacred mantra," it is admitted, "is fashioned in the heart" (I.67.2) as thought emerging from the realm of truth becomes visible through its lustre and audible as it is sounded. The "bringing to birth within the heart of a thought as light" (III.26.8) is caused by Agni, the divine flame, "immortal guest in mortal bodies," hidden "in the cave of the heart whom men find when they have sung their prayers, fashioned in the heart" (I.67.2).

We have thus three remarkable elements in this Vedic Science of the Word, this Rg Veda (Rg=word, veda= knowledge, science, wisdom):

(1) The peculiarly evocative power of words;
(2) Every sound vibration manifests as light;
(3) The mantra originates in the innermost centre, the heart.

It is therefore that truth which wells forth from the heart as inspiration, taking form through sound and light and becoming objective as the word, or combination of words, the word made visible, made palpable, "made flesh" (Secret Doctrine).

Within the heart is born the vision, the thought, the truth, within the heart it is translated into the appropriate words, hence the sacredness of those words. So the poets are described as bearing the light within their mouth, for their utterances are inspired, just as they are said to be sun-eyed since they reflect the divine light from within their heart into their eyes. Golden tongued and sun-eyed, these are the holy bards of ancient India, the light-bringers. The most famous mantra of the Rgveda which is said to contain the essence of the Vedas is the Gayatri. It is an invocation to the Lord of solar splendour that He may pierce through our visionary thought, that we may receive His light.

II. Visual Meditation was absorption in the light emitted either by sound or thought, for thought itself is a manifestation of light. The wielding of thought as an instrument of power was the special achievement of the sages. Patañjali, in his Yoga-sutras, only codified what they had fathomed ages before his time. With the Vedic sages, thought which for

Patañjali was a modification of the thinking principle, was regarded as a lens to be focussed upon the would-be object of meditation, leading to actual vision and to actual entering into contact with other fields of consciousness and to the discovery of their own denizens, their own laws and their meaning. So the seers, we are told.

"harness their minds, harness their thoughts" (V.81.1)

as though these were steeds; with homage they yoke the ancient power of the spirit and compare this lens to a boat or chariot "not made for horses or for reins" (IV.36.2) whereby they cross over to the other shore and penetrate into the region where the "shining ones" are masters, the devas whose "lower habitations are perceived (but who themselves abide in remoter, hidden dominions" (III.54.5), that region whose root is the seat of truth, *rta*, the divine cosmic harmony whence issue all the gods, to which are traced all divine statutes which the gods themselves obey. The Vedic vision, reflecting that harmony, "shining from the realm of truth" (X.III.2) was "born of truth".

Thus it is that the bards investigated the great law of the universe, the law of cosmic order, or equilibrium and all those laws that derive therefrom; thus it is that they penetrated into the secret of death and investigated the states of consciousness of after-death life, discovered its meaning and the significance of immortality.

III. The science of seership, of light and the sacred word, should lead us to the apex of the soul, the spirit. A striking metaphor used by the bards shows them as vultures that for days circle round their prey which turns out to be none other than that inspired or illumined vision for which the poet longed, which he fashions into a prayer and by means of which he pushes open the fountain lid of immortality. Immortality is the essence of that flame-spirit in which man loses himself to find his greater Self. The inner senses should lead him to his flame-spirit, as they did with the Vedic bards, and not to the illusory and dangerous intoxication of psychic powers.

With perception of the heart—in Vedic language the heart is the soul—the sages were able to penetrate into the "secret of the thousand-branched tree" of life (VII.33.9) and in their "heart-searching meditation" they discovered "the bond between the created and the Uncreate" (X.129.4), the relationship between God and man. We touch here upon that ground of the soul whence even visualization itself is transcended, when vision transmutes itself into something which the mind cannot grasp for it lies beyond its province. It borders on the flame-spirit. In deep absorption the sages crossed beyond the dividing line that separates the known from the unknown, the soul from the spirit, and penetrated into that state whence the spirit, the power of the unborn, flashes forth a moment and fills the meditator's whole being with knowledge, with illumination. Then it is that the Vedic seer entered into the "fourth degree of prayer" when the "Lordly herdsman of the whole universe, the enlightened One entered into me, the simple" (I.164.21).

Here is the height and depth of Vedic seership. In the exaltation of the revelation the poet sang:

> "I have known this mighty divine man,
> refulgent as the sun beyond darkness,
> only by knowing him does one overcome death.
> No other way is there to go." (Yajurveda.)

In the illumination of that "loftier light beyond the darkness" he realized that from the furthest stars right to our own innermost heart, throbs that same dynamic pulse, the fire of the spirit that maketh all things new, he found "The One whose shadow is death whose shadow is immortality" (X.121.3).

This is indeed the "flight from the alone to the Alone."

These pages are provided for notes which the reader may wish to make on these remarkable Scripts.